AfterLife

AfterLife

WHAT YOU NEED TO KNOW ABOUT HEAVEN, THE HEREAFTER & NEAR-DEATH EXPERIENCES

HANK HANEGRAAFF

WORTHY
PUBLISHING

Published by Worthy Publishing, a division of Worthy Media, Inc., 134 Franklin Road, Suite 200, Brentwood, Tennessee 37027.

HELPING PEOPLE EXPERIENCE THE HEART OF GOD

eBook available at www.worthypublishing.com

Audio book distributed through Brilliance Audio; visit www.brillianceaudio.com

Library of Congress Control Number: 2012950269

Before reading the book, you may find it helpful to look at the glossary for explanations of terms that may be unfamiliar.

For foreign and subsidiary rights, contact Riggins International Rights Service, Inc., www.rigginsrights.com

ISBN: 978-1-61795-081-0 (hardcover w/jacket)
ISBN: 978-1-61795-208-1 (international trade papaer)
Cover Design: Christopher Tobias, Tobias' Outerwear for Books
Cover Image: © Neo Edmund/Fotolia
Interior Design and Typesetting: Kimberly Sagmiller, Fudge Creative

Printed in the United States of America

13 14 15 16 17 18 LBM 8 7 6 5 4 3 2 1

To Paul Stephen—
a son who puts a smile on my face
and a healthy dose of pride in my heart

CONTENTS

⋮

PART ONE
Life *after* Life-after-Life: The Eternal Heaven and Earth

⋮

PART TWO
Life after Life: The Transitional Heaven

⋮

PART THREE
Life: What You Do Now Counts for All Eternity

FOREWORD

My wife, Leslie, walked into our bedroom one August night—and there she saw me, unconscious on the floor. She immediately called the paramedics, and I vaguely remember being loaded into the ambulance. At the hospital, I was sufficiently conscious for the physician's words to register with full force: "You're one step away from a coma, two steps away from dying."

A cascade of medical issues had put me on the edge of death. And I can tell you from personal experience that at times like this the subject of the afterlife is more than just a dry academic topic. When you might very well be on the verge of leaving this world, it becomes critically urgent to know what awaits you in the next.

By God's grace, I was released from the hospital after more than a week of intensive treatment, and today my overall health has been restored. But that frightening episode was a stark reminder that someday I will close my eyes for the final time in this world. What will happen when I reopen them? And how about you: what will you face when you pass from this existence into the one that follows?

My friend Hank Hanegraaff provides clear, concise, and compelling answers to questions like these in his book *AfterLife*. He explores the topics that typically befuddle people, such as: Is there really a heaven? Is so, what will it be like? What about hell? Is the popular portrayal of fire and brimstone accurate? Is there such a place as purgatory? Most important of all, how can I know for sure that I will be in the presence of God forever?

Building on a strong foundation of biblical teaching, Hank covers these questions as well as an impressive array of related subjects, ranging from whether ghosts are real (don't bet on it); whether near-death experiences reveal anything certain about eternity (not so much); and even whether we will enjoy sex in heaven (you'll have to read the book!).

While a few issues in this book fall outside my scope of expertise, such as how the end times will unfold, I always find Hank's perspective to be provocative and worthy of full consideration.

Let's face it: nothing is more important or relevant than how you will spend eternity. Rather than traffic in speculation or unanchored opinions, Hank consistently turns to the Book that offers the ultimate answers. As he does on his *Bible Answer Man* radio program, Hank measures his answers by the teachings of Scripture—and then he explains them in terms that each of us can understand and apply.

I don't want to spoil the ending, but there's good news in this book: hope is available to each of us through Christ! As you journey toward that encouraging conclusion, you'll find cogent responses to many of your pressing questions about the world to come.

As someone who came within two steps of death, I'm thrilled to know there are answers that will calm our minds—and satisfy our souls.

—LEE STROBEL
AUTHOR, *THE CASE FOR CHRIST* AND *THE CASE FOR FAITH*

Someday you will die— then what?

Aim at Heaven and you will get earth "thrown in"; aim at earth and you will get neither.

—C. S. LEWIS

You and I are designed to live forever.

Put another way, death is not the end. Death is, in reality, entrance into a brand-new sphere of existence. For like the caterpillar, we will be transformed. The analogy is both breathtaking and instructive. For though the caterpillar dies, yet will it live. Indeed, its chrysalis is in essence a casket in which the caterpillar experiences both ruin and resurrection. During this intermediate phase, constituent parts devolve into a mysterious molecular mixture. Then the extraordinary happens: eyes that once could only distinguish between light and darkness are transformed into majestic orbs with a field of vision and color acuity that exceeds our own. Wings appear as if by magic. An indescribably complex reproductive system—wholly absent in the caterpillar—emerges mysteriously. An unimaginable strawlike proboscis emerges, allowing the resurrected creature to indulge in the nectar of a brand-new life. The transformed being that emerges is simply beyond belief!

Correspondence to our death and resurrection is remarkable. For, like the caterpillar, we, too, will experience a majestic metamorphosis through three distinct phases of life.

First, there is life in the present. When your mother conceived you she did not merely conceive your body; she conceived both the physical and the metaphysical aspects of your humanity. From the moment you were knit together in your mother's womb you manifested all the criteria of biological life, including metabolism, development, cell reproduction, and the ability to react to stimuli. Moreover, you were endowed by your Creator with a distinct genetic code. Though your personality was far from fully developed, you were fully a person from the moment of your conception. From that moment to the moment of death you can rightly be said to be experiencing the nectar of life. But death is not the end!

Furthermore, there is *life* after life. At some future point in time, you and I will experience the separation of the physical and nonphysical aspects of our humanity. My father, who died in 1997, is currently experiencing this transitional phase. To borrow the words of the apostle Paul, my father is now "away from the body and at home with the Lord" (2 Corinthians 5:8). In other words, he is even now experiencing *life* after life. To say that the *life* after life that my father now experiences is extraordinary is to understate reality. Paul goes so far as to say that "to depart and be with Christ" is actually "better by far" (Philippians 1:23). Disembodied, my father no longer experiences *whereness* (extension in space); his *awareness*, however, has been greatly magnified.

Finally, there is life *after* life-after-life. My father, then, is poised to experience yet another phase of existence. Indeed, this is the very quintessence of the Christian worldview. Jesus died and was physically resurrected. And so it will be for you and me. As Jesus rose, we, too, will rise. While the Christian worldview does not necessitate that every atom will be resuscitated in resurrection, it does underscore continuity between our earthly body and our eternal body. "So will it be at the resurrection of the dead" says Paul. "The body that is sown is perishable, it is raised imperishable; it is sown in dishonor, it is raised in glory; it is sown in weakness, it is raised in power; it is sown a natural body, it is raised a spiritual body" (1 Corinthians 15:42–44). As such, when Jesus appears a second time, the nonphysical aspect of my father's humanity—now "at home with the Lord"—will be reunited with a real, physical, flesh-and-bone body, perfectly engineered for "a new heaven and a new earth" (Revelation 21:1). Like the butterfly, he will be changed! In a moment, in the twinkling of an eye, he will be transformed! As a caterpillar is transformed into a butterfly, so our resurrected body will be numerically identical to the body we now possess. In other words, our resurrection body is not a second body; rather, it is our present body transformed.

This of course raises a lot of questions. If heaven is for real, who gets to go there? Does heaven have pearly gates and streets of gold? What happens to those who have never heard of Jesus? Do people in heaven know what is presently happening on earth? How old will we be in eternity? What about ghosts? Is hell for real? Do demons torment the damned there? And what about pets?

A host of related questions are no doubt percolating in your mind as you ponder these three stages of life. Unfortunately, many such questions are presently being answered by faulty interpretations of Scripture, by out-of-body experiences, and now—as detailed in chapter 7—through the popular craze of near-death experiences (NDEs).

In the 1975 multimillion bestseller *Life after Life*, Raymond Moody, widely considered to be the father of NDEs, provides a poignant portrayal of unconditional love and universal acceptance emanating from the frontier between this world and the next. Gone are portrayals of reward and punishment in the hereafter, replaced by transcendental experiences so enlivening that returning to the body is tantamount to death by comparison.[1]

In 1992 Betty Eadie's popular *Embraced by the Light* cracked open the divide between death and the afterlife to millions more. Beyond death's door she experienced a divine light more brilliant than the sun. She recognized the light as the very Jesus she had known in preexistence long before she experienced life on earth. As her light merged with the divine she felt an utter explosion of love and enlightenment. It was there she discovered that Eve had not fallen to temptation but had made a conscious decision to bring about the conditions necessary for progression to godhood.[2]

In 2004 Baptist pastor Don Piper added to the ever-growing corpus of information on life after life after his own resurrection from the dead. "Now," writes Pastor Piper in his *90 Minutes in Heaven*, "I can speak authoritatively about heaven from firsthand knowledge."[3] Among Piper's firsthand discoveries were that the streets of heaven were really gold[4] and that those who walked them were "old and young and every age in-between."[5] In fact, says Piper, "All of the people I encountered were the same age they had been last time I had seen them."[6] His grandfather still had the same "shock of white hair" and "big banana nose."[7] Most notably, as Piper revealed to a worldwide Christian television audience, because he has already died—and people only die once—Jesus will return within his very own lifetime.[8]

In 2006 Bill Wiese became a *New York Times* best-selling author with the release of *23 Minutes in Hell*. Unlike the apostle Paul—who did not know whether he was in the body or apart from the body (2 Corinthians 12:1–6)—God revealed to Bill that his twenty-three-minute trip involved a bona fide out-of-body experience. In hell, Wiese uncovered a wealth of extrabiblical information, including temperature (300 degrees/zero humidity); the location (center of the earth); reptilian-looking demons (some of whom are fifteen feet tall) who rule over and torture humans; rats the size of dogs; and snakes as big as trains.[9]

Even newer revelations concerning life after life arrived in 2010 with the publication of *Heaven Is for Real: A Little Boy's Astounding Story of His Trip to Heaven and Back.* In this multimillion publishing phenomenon—which stayed at #1 on the *New York Times* Best Seller List an astonishing forty-four consecutive weeks—Wesleyan pastor Todd Burpo tells the story of how his son Colton endured the equivalent of a near-death experience. Speaking "with the simple conviction of an eyewitness" Colton reveals a God who looks like Gabriel, only larger, has blue eyes, yellow hair, and huge wings; a Jesus with sea-green-bluish eyes, brown hair, no wings, but with a rainbow-colored horse; and a Holy Spirit who is bluish but hard to see.[10] In addition to interacting with the triune God during his three minutes in heaven, the three-year-old was afforded an opportunity to meet a host of biblical luminaries including John the Baptist, Samson, David, Peter, John the son of Zebedee, and the archangel Gabriel.[11] Not only did he meet these Bible heroes, but as a direct "eyewitness" of heaven Colton was empowered to settle theological issues the church has struggled with throughout its history, received revelation superseding that of biblical prophets and apostles, and "had also been shown the future."[12]

The quintessential near-death experience, however, did not surface until the 2012 mega-best-selling publication of *Proof of Heaven: A Neurosurgeons's Journey into the Afterlife.* "As arrogant as that might sound," writes Dr. Eben Alexander, "I was allowed to die harder, and travel deeper, than almost all NDE subjects before me." Indeed, says Dr. Alexander, "mine was in some ways a perfect storm of near-death experiences . . . a technically near-impeccable near-death experience, perhaps one of the most convincing such cases in modern history." And through it he finally "understood what religion was really all about": "You are loved and cherished, dearly, forever." "You have nothing to fear." "There is nothing you can do wrong." "This," writes Alexander, "is not only the single most important emotional truth in the universe, but also the single most important *scientific* truth as well."[13] The implications, of course, are profound. No matter what someone does in this life, the single greatest truth is that unconditional love and joy awaits them in the life to come. Such is no doubt solace for the impenitent. After murdering his mother, twenty children, and six adults in the Sandy Hook Elementary School massacre in Connecticut, Adam Lanza murders himself and simply soars off on what Alexander romanticizes as "the wing of a butterfly."[14]

Moreover, the "unconditionally loving God" he encountered during his near-death experience enabled Alexander to understand he was "part of the Divine." Remarkably, by way of the Orb (Alexander's personal guide and interpreter), "Om" (God) revealed mysteries that lie far beyond the reach of modern-day science and learning. "Through the Orb, Om told me that there is not one universe but many—in fact, more than I could conceive." Not only so, but as revealed by Om, "the universe has no beginning or end."[15]

In short, while subscribing to the reality that there is life after life, books such as Alexander's *Proof of Heaven* and Burpo's *Heaven Is for Real* paint entirely different and conflicting portraits of the afterlife. For Burpo, Jesus and his rainbow-colored pony are central. For Alexander, it is Om and the Orb. Indeed, had Alexander not discovered that the Orb was his birth sister Betsy, he may well have doubted the authenticity of "the whole new worldview" he was slowly building "and thus of the true existence of that entire realm."[16]

Time and space permitting, many more revelations from beyond death's door could be cited. For example, long before Bill Wiese had his hellish out-of-body experience, Jesus personally directed Mary K. Baxter on a forty-day tour of hell. In her best seller titled *A Divine Revelation of Hell*, she tells of a place deep within the earth, shaped like a human being, where snakes and rats dwell, and where worms slither through ignited corpses.[17] And subsequent to three-year-old Colton Burpo's return from heaven, six-year-old Alex Malarkey traveled there as well. In the gripping *New York Times* bestseller titled *The Boy Who Came back from Heaven: A Remarkable Account of Miracles, Angels, and Life beyond This World*, Alex and his father, Kevin, tell "a true story" of "Alex's direct experience with angels, demons, and, yes, the devil himself."[18] Along the way he encountered "one hundred and fifty pure, white angels with fantastic wings,"[19] green demons with long fingernails and hair made of fire, and an earless devil, replete with three heads, a nasty nose, and moldy teeth. Like Colton, Alex was permitted to see God. But in sharp distinction, he was not permitted to see God's face. Says Alex, "I was in the presence of God. He had a body that was like a human body, but it was a lot bigger. I could only see up to His neck because, like the Bible says, nobody is allowed to see God's face or that person will die."[20]

And therein lies the dilemma. The subjective recollections of those who experience heaven via NDEs are wildly divergent—and seemingly informed by their preconceptions. Raymond Moody's fixation on an eternity devoid of judgment is compatible with his occult predilections. Betty Eadie's recognition of Jesus from life in the preexistence is consistent with her Mormon beliefs and background. Don Piper's claim that Jesus will return within his own lifetime harmonizes well with his end-time presuppositions. Bill Wiese's notion of reptilian-looking demons commissioned to torture humans as the caretakers of hell is consistent with medieval folklore and superstition. The Burpos' extrabiblical revelations comport well with modern-day prophets who routinely foretell the future. Eben Alexander's flights with "the Girl on the Butterfly Wing" [21] align with his evolutionary preconceptions and his marginalization of sin and the need for the Savior. And, of course, the Malarkeys' description of the Father with a humanlike body and a devil with three heads fits well with modern sensibilities respecting the ontology of God and angels.

Furthermore, there is the ever-lurking danger of hyperliteralism. Those reporting firsthand observations of heaven and hell are often predisposed to interpret the Bible literalistically. Therefore, it is not surprising that they return from the afterlife with stories of gates made of genuine pearl and streets manufactured from the purest of gold. And such stories are not without precedent. Popular books on heaven are replete with similar statements. It is not uncommon to see heaven described as a translucent cube measuring fifteen hundred miles in each direction (Revelation 21:15–16).[22] While the authors may genuinely suppose their interpretations to be in harmony with Scripture, they appear to be at odds with the art and science of biblical interpretation—not to mention plain old common sense. As I seek to underscore in the pages that follow, the imagery of Revelation is not intended to tell us what heaven looks like but rather is intended to tell us what heaven *is* like.

When John describes Jesus as a lion and a lamb he is using imagery that even casual readers of Scripture are intimately acquainted with. This is likewise so with the imagery of gold, precious stones, and pearls. Their luminous beauty is repugnant when associated with the extreme wickedness of a harlot city "glittering with gold, precious stones and pearls" (Revelation 18:16) yet resplendent when associated with the extravagant wisdom and wealth of the Holy City coming down out of heaven from God (Revelation 21)—the harlot city an obvious parody of the Holy City. Such is likewise the case when it comes to heaven's description as a cube. Its measurement is not only parodied by the length and width of mystery Babylon (the ancient Roman Empire) but as with the cube shape of the Holy of Holies in which Jehovah dwelled, Jerusalem, imagined as a cube, will forever be the dwelling place of God. Says John, "Now the dwelling of God is with men, and he will live with them. They will be his people and God himself will be with them and be their God" (Revelation 21:3).

Finally, there is the very real issue of apostolic authority. God himself set the conditions by which new revelations must be ratified—namely, confirmation by those who were eyewitnesses to the resurrection of Jesus Christ. Thus with the death of the apostles there can be no new revelations—much less new revelations that compromise, confuse, or outright contradict "the faith once for all delivered to the saints" (Jude 3). Paul is the quintessential test case. The apostolic community validated him as an eyewitness to the resurrection and as an apostle. Thus, revelation received through the apostle Paul—unlike revelations received through modern revelators—may be deemed reliable and binding on the body of Christ.

Let me be clear. I do not doubt that those mentioned above had actual subjective experiences. But that is precisely the point. Subjective experiences are notoriously unreliable; thus, they must always be tested in light of an objective frame of reference—which in Christianity is the Bible. Colton Burpo may genuinely believe that God has yellow hair and big wings. But we do well to "test everything. Hold on to the good" (1 Thessalonians 5:21).

As you dig in, let me remind you again of the transcendent significance of the topic at hand. All of us will spend eternity somewhere. It stands to reason, therefore, that we know precisely what that entails.

A television ad caught my attention as I was running on the treadmill just this morning. The narrator claimed that we humans only get twenty-five thousand mornings, more or less. This, however, is hardly true. The reality is, the redeemed will live forever in renewed bodies perfectly suited for a restored universe. Like the butterfly, we will experience what the caterpillar could not. In Eden restored our bodies and souls will fly full and free, unfettered by the stain of selfishness and sin.

Read on! And prepare to be inspired.

PART ONE

. . .

Life *after* Life-after-Life:
The Eternal Heaven and Earth

An all-too-common misconception regarding the afterlife is that it entails only one phase. In truth there is much more. As explained earlier, a biblical worldview includes three phases of life—not only this life, but also life after life, followed by life *after* life-after-life.

First, you experience *life*. Your life on earth began at the moment a microscopic egg in your mother's womb was fertilized by a particular sperm cell emanating from your father. That union not only marked the beginning of your life but the genetic future your life would have. A single fertilized egg (zygote) the size of a pinhead contains chemical instructions that would fill more than five hundred thousand printed pages. The genetic information contained in your "encyclopedia" determines every potential physical aspect of your development from height to hair color. But you are more than just physical. You were not only conceived as a body; you were conceived as a body/soul unity. Put another way, both the physical and the nonphysical aspects of your humanity were present at the moment of your conception.

Furthermore, just as there is life, there is *life after life*. At some future point in time, you will experience an unnatural rending of body and soul. Your body will return to the ground from whence it came, but your soul will continue to have conscious existence apart from the body. As Jesus assured the repentant thief dying on a cross next to him, "I tell you the truth, today you will be with me in paradise" (Luke 23:43). Likewise after the death of Lazarus in Luke 16, Jesus describes him as being conscious in the presence of God. To borrow the words of the apostle Paul, he was "away from the body and at home with the Lord" (2 Corinthians 5:8). Disembodied, he no longer experienced *whereness* (extension in space); his *awareness*, however, was greatly intensified. Thus, it may well be said that Lazarus is presently experiencing life after life.

Finally, you will experience *life* after *life-after-life* when "the time comes for God to restore everything" (Acts 3:21). A great deal of confusion surrounds the transitional state (a state my father even now is experiencing) and the eternal state, which can be experienced only after Jesus appears a second time. At that time the soul of my father, who died as a follower of Christ in 1997, will return to his body. Then my father will once again be fully human—that is to say, a body/soul unity. Likewise, those who are alive at Christ's second coming will experience a metamorphosis equivalent to death and resurrection.

Like the caterpillar whose constituent parts dissolve into a molecular soup and then reemerge in new and better fashion, the mortal will be clothed with all of the wonders of immortality. "When the perishable has been clothed with the imperishable, and the mortal with immortality, then the saying that is written will come true: 'Death has been swallowed up in victory'" (1 Corinthians 15:54).

We begin in part 1 with the apex of existence: that of life *after* life-after-life in the eternal heaven and earth. At present there is, as it were, a veil that separates the habitation of God from the habitation of humanity. In the redemption of all things, that veil will be removed and sacred space will fill our place.

In part 2 we delve directly into life after life in the transitional heaven. My goal is to provide you with crystal clarity regarding that which happens at the moment of death. This is particularly crucial in that the current craze surrounding near-death experiences has greatly clouded our perceptions regarding life after life.

Finally, in part 3 we come face-to-face with the significance of the present life. You and I as yet live between the inauguration of the kingdom of heaven and the consummation when heaven and earth will be joined as one. In the meantime we are called to be mediators by which this present world may be transformed. As such, what we do now counts for all eternity.

CHAPTER
ONE

⋮

What is heaven about?

WHAT IS HEAVEN?

To be resurrected for the life of heaven is the true Christian hope. As life in the "intermediate" or "interim" state between death and resurrection is better than the life in this world that preceded it, so the life of resurrection will be better still. It will, in fact, be best. And this is what God has in store for all his children. Hallelujah!

—J. I. PACKER

The biblical story of redemption is rooted in the tree of life. In the beginning the tree of life appears as the centerpiece of the Edenic garden. On the far side of history, it reappears in the eternal garden. In between, it stands on Golgotha's hill as the fulcrum of human history. On it, God-made-flesh stretches one hand toward the garden of Eden, the other toward the eternal garden. The immortality the first Adam could no longer reach, the Second Adam touched in his place. He vanquished the power of evil and gave ultimate victory to the knowledge of good. As descendants of Adam, we can as yet embrace the tree of life where the personification of all that is good took all that is evil upon himself. In other words, you and I can experience heaven. The question is, what exactly does that mean?

First, heaven is the *experience of eternal life*—the polar opposite of eternal death. Death is what the parents of humanity experienced when they ate from the fruit of the tree of the knowledge of good and evil. In accordance with God's warning, they were driven from Paradise and experienced what it meant to be alienated from their Creator. In place of eternal life they experienced spiritual death, and creation itself experienced the reality of groaning in travail.

Post-Paradise, the Bible chronicles an unfolding plan of redemption by which our human parents, their posterity, and Paradise itself might be brought back into right relationship with their Maker. A plan of redemption by which earth and earthlings would once again experience wholeness. A time in which "the earth will be filled with the knowledge of the glory of the Lord, as the waters cover the sea" (Habakkuk 2:14). A time in which earthlings will be fulfilled in knowledge and relationship to God. "This is eternal life," wrote the Apostle of Love, "that they may know you, the only true God, and Jesus Christ, whom you have sent" (John 17:3).

The Apostle to the Gentiles summed up the essence of eternal life brilliantly: "As in Adam all die, so in Christ all will be made alive" (1 Corinthians 15:22). Indeed, writes John, Christ *is* "eternal life" (1 John 5:20). Everlasting destruction is to be "shut out from the presence of the Lord and from the majesty of his power" (2 Thessalonians 1:9); conversely, eternal life is to experience what Adam and Eve once knew when they walked with God in the cool of the day.

Furthermore, heaven is the *eternal expression of the image of God*. From the fall onward the goal of redemption is the restoration of God's image in fallen humanity. As such, the imago Dei tarnished in the fall is to be transformed in the forever: "Just as we have borne the likeness of the earthly man, so shall we bear the likeness of the man from heaven" (1 Corinthians 15:49). Put another way, the redeemed will—in perfection—eternally bear the image of God in heaven.

Think about it this way. Christ is the image of the invisible God, and Christ-*ians* are progressively being conformed to the image of Christ. When "Philip said, 'Lord, show us the Father and that will be enough for us,' Jesus answered, "Don't you know me, Philip, even after I have been among you such a long time? Anyone who has seen me has seen the Father'" (John 14:8–9). In other words, Jesus is "the radiance of God's glory and the exact representation of his being" (Hebrews 1:3). And as Christ "is the image of the invisible God, the firstborn over all creation" (Colossians 1:15), Christians are "predestined to be conformed to the likeness of his Son, that he might be the firstborn among many brothers" (Romans 8:29).

What that means from a practical standpoint is that through

sanctification God is renewing an image that as yet is blemished and broken. And when Jesus appears a second time, "we shall be like him, for we shall see him as he is" (1 John 3:2). The image of God now distorted will then be divine. Christ-*ians* will bear the image of God patterned after Christ—the true imago Dei.

Finally, heaven is quite literally the *Easter of earth*—the moment that all creation yearns for. The hope of Christianity is not only that God will resurrect our physical carcasses but that he will redeem the physical cosmos. Christ will not resurrect an entirely different group of human beings; rather, he will resurrect the very people who throughout history have populated this planet. In like manner, God will not renew another cosmos; rather, he will redeem the very world he once called "very good" (Genesis 1:31). As such, the Easter of earth is the transformation of the cosmos.

What happens to our physical carcasses and what happens to the physical cosmos go hand in hand. Together they will be redeemed, restored, and resurrected. Paul elucidates it eloquently. The very creation which is at present "groaning as in the pains of childbirth" will, at the second appearance of Christ, "be liberated from its bondage to decay." Likewise, "we ourselves, who have the firstfruits of the Spirit, groan inwardly as we eagerly await our adoption as sons, the redemption of our bodies" (Romans 8:18–25). As Christ emerged from the tomb of Easter, so a new cosmos will emerge from the womb of earth.

It is incredible to think that one day soon we will not only experience the resurrection of our carcasses but the renewal of the cosmos and the return of the Creator. We will literally experience heaven on earth. Eden lost will become Eden restored and a whole lot more. The veil between heaven and earth will be vanquished and Jesus will appear in a new heaven and a new earth wherein righteousness dwells. Heaven and earth will no longer be separated but will be united as one glorious domain—a domain in which we will experience eternal life, eternally express the image of God, and bask in the Easter of earth.

WHERE IS HEAVEN?

The early Christians hold firmly to a two-step belief about the future: first, death and whatever lies immediately beyond; second, a new bodily existence in a newly remade world.

—N. T. WRIGHT

Ask a Christian where heaven is and the inevitable answer is that it is somewhere up there. If you travel upward from the perspective of Jerusalem (downward from Tonga) you will inevitably encounter a heavenly city. Some say that city measures two and a quarter million miles square and has a wall two hundred and sixteen feet wide and seven million feet high, twelve gates made of single pearls, foundations constructed from a variety of precious stones, and a singular street that is literally pure gold. Upon their return, many near-deathers speak of being received thorough pearly gates and running on pure gold. It is, they say, precisely as described by the Apostle of the Apocalypse. But is that true? Is heaven really up there somewhere? Does it really have a street of gold? And if so, how exactly do we get there?

First, from a biblical perspective we may rightly say that heaven is where God is. As we have seen, to be "away from the body" is to be "home with the Lord" (2 Corinthians 5:8). While this is a profound reality, it is not at present a physical reality. Only when Jesus appears a second time will physical bodies be resurrected. In the meantime, the immaterial souls of those who have died in faith are even now, as Jesus described it, at "Abraham's side" (Luke 16:22).

This, of course, is not a *locational* promise; it is a *relational* promise. Indeed, to ask *where* Abraham's side is reduces our Lord's words to an absurdity. While souls most certainly have *awareness*, they do not have *whereness*. Put another way, nonphysical souls do not have extension in space. Therefore, asking for the physical location of a soul is a category mistake. The language Scripture employs to communicate where God is should be regarded as a heavenly condescension by which heavenly realities are conveyed through the *lingua franca* of earth.

When my father died in 1997, we buried his body in a cemetery in Michigan. Not so the nonphysical aspect of his humanity. His non-material soul is even now where God is. He once prayed, "Our Father which art in heaven" (Matthew 6:9 KJV). He is now in that very space. The best, however, is yet to come. For one day, "the Lord himself will come down from heaven, with a loud command, with the voice of the archangel and with the trumpet call of God and the dead in Christ will rise first" (1 Thessalonians 4:16). On that day, his soul will reemerge in a resurrected body that is immortal and imperishable. In the meantime, he, along with "a great cloud of witnesses" (Hebrews 12:1), is enjoying the presence of God.

Furthermore, heaven is where we are. For heaven is not a place alto-gether other than this universe; rather, it is this universe restored. If God annihilated the present cosmos, Satan would have won a decisive victory. The Bible, however, knows of no such thing. Satan is defeated and the full measure of his defeat will be evidenced when a corrupted cosmos groaning in travail will be liberated from its bondage to disease, destruction, decay, and death itself.

That, ultimately, is the hope of Christianity: the resurrection of our physical bodies and the renewal of the physical universe, includ-ing earth. The grand and glorious promise of the biblical worldview is that we will once again walk this physical planet. Therefore, when the apostles Peter and John speak of "a new heaven and a new earth" (2 Peter 3:13; Revelation 21:1), they are describing a universe that, though renewed, stands in continuity with the one we presently inhabit. In other words, at the second appearing of our Lord and Savior Jesus Christ this universe will be thoroughly transformed as opposed to totally terminated.

Just as there is continuity between our present body and our res-urrected body, so too there will be continuity between the physical universe and the one we will inhabit throughout eternity. Again the caterpillar is instructive. In the chrysalis it experiences ruin and then resurrection. Though its constituent parts dissolve into a mysterious molecular mixture, out of the ruins a butterfly springs forth in resurrection. So it will be with the present creation. Its elements will "melt in the heat. But in keeping with his promise we are looking forward to a new heaven and a new earth, the home of righteousness" (2 Peter 3:12–13). Though the elements will be destroyed by fire, like a mother in labor, the present cosmos will give birth to a perfect creation in which "there will be no more death or mourning or crying or pain, for the old order of things has passed away. He who was seated on the throne said, 'I am making everything new!'" (Revelation 21:3–5).

Finally, we might rightly say that heaven is where God is *and* where we are. At present there is, as it were, a veil that separates the habitation of God from the habitation of humanity. In the redemption of all things, that veil will be removed. Christ will then be available to us physically as he now is available to us spiritually. The Shekinah glory that once filled Solomon's temple will fill the new heavens and the new earth. When the veil is removed, "the earth will be filled with the knowledge of the glory of the Lord as the waters cover the sea" (Habakkuk 2:14). Sacred space will fill our place.

Bethel, an ordinary place, became sacred space when Yahweh, the Creator of the heavens and the earth, appeared to the father of true Israel. Suddenly that which was ordinary became extraordinary. Bethel was transformed into the sacred space of God. "Surely," exuded Jacob, "this is none other than the house of God; this is the gate of heaven" (Genesis 28:16–17). Mount Sinai likewise became sacred space when Moses there encountered God's glory. "To the Israelites the glory of the Lord looked like a consuming fire on top of the mountain" (Exodus 24:17), for a glimpse of glory had been unveiled. Joshua encountered sacred space when he neared Jericho. Thus, the commander of the Lord's army said to him, "Take off your sandals, for the place where you are standing is holy" (Joshua 5:15). The garden of Eden, of course, was the quintessential sacred space. For there it was that God walked with the parents of humanity in the cool of the day.

All of this is but a portrait of what will be when the veil, between where God is and where we are, is permanently removed. Moses trembled in fear when he encountered sacred space at the burning bush (Exodus 3). Likewise, when the prophet Isaiah, the holiest man in Israel, "saw the Lord, high and exalted, seated on a throne; and the train of his robe filled the temple," he cried out, "Woe to me! . . . I am ruined! For I am a man of unclean lips and I live among a people of unclean lips, and my eyes have seen the King, the LORD Almighty" (Isaiah 6:1–5). Yet when God's space and ours merge, all such terror will be no more. Our lips will be cleansed. Our hearts will be purified. We will touch the sacred mountain, the heavenly Jerusalem, without as much as a tinge of fear. We will "come to thousands upon thousands of angels in joyful assembly, to the church of the firstborn, whose names are written in heaven. You have come to God" (Hebrews 12:22–23).

So where is heaven? Is it up there somewhere? A place made of jasper with pearly gates and a street of pure gold? Heavens, no! The language is a heavenly condescension to our earthly inadequacies. Revelation's descriptions are not intended to communicate what heaven *looks* like any more than hair "white like wool, as white as snow" is intended to tell us what Jesus looks like (1:14). Rather, such descriptions are intended to communicate what heaven *is* like. As with the golden bowls full of incense (prayers of the saints); the golden lampstands (churches); and fine linen (righteous acts of the saints); so the metaphors describing the heavenly city magnify a far more majestic and glorious reality. A reality far grander than a fourteen-hundred-cubic-mile[1] Jerusalem constructed of jewels and jasper.

No! Heaven involves our earth—these fields, these mountains, these rivers, our space—united as one with the glory of God. It is God's sacred space and our purified place a glorious whole. "For the Lord himself will come down from heaven, with a loud command, with the voice of the archangel and with the trumpet call of God" (1 Thessalonians 4:16). "No longer will there be any curse. The throne of God and of the Lamb will be in the city, and his servants will serve him. They will see his face, and his name will be on their foreheads. There will be no more night. They will not need the light of a lamp or the light of the sun, for the Lord God will give them light. And they will reign for ever and ever" (Revelation 22:3–5).

WHEN DO WE RECEIVE OUR RESURRECTED BODIES?

I know he will rise again in the resurrection at the last day.
—MARTHA, SISTER OF LAZARUS, WHOM CHRIST RAISED FROM THE DEAD

The question of when we receive resurrected bodies is one I encountered frequently after the death of my father. Family members and friends wanted to know whether my dad had become a disembodied soul or whether he received his resurrection body the moment he died.

First, Scripture clearly refers to the moment of death as disembodiment, not re-embodiment. In his second letter to the Corinthians, Paul makes it crystal clear that to be "at home with the Lord" is to be "away from the body" and to be "away from the body" is to be "at home with the Lord" (5:6, 8).

The notion that believers receive temporary bodies during the intermediate state is either ad hoc or atrocious hermeneutics. Nowhere does the Bible explicitly tell us that upon death we assume temporary bodies. Those who suppose such things turn Scripture into a wax nose. One writer goes as far as to suggest that the martyrs in heaven were given fine linen to wear; thus, they must also have had temporary bodies. What is not mentioned is that the Apostle of the Apocalypse specifically defines "fine linen" as "the righteous acts of the saints" (Revelation 19:8). In like fashion, he defines "golden bowls full of incense" as "the prayers of the saints" (5:8).

Furthermore, Scripture teaches that believers are not resurrected until the second coming of Christ. Paul explicitly says that when the Lord comes down from heaven, "the dead in Christ will rise first" (1 Thessalonians 4:16). Jesus himself taught that at his coming bodily return to earth "all who are in their graves will hear his voice and come out—those who have done good will rise to live, and those who have done evil will rise to be condemned" (John 5:28–29).

If believers received their resurrected bodies at the moment of death, they obviously could not receive them at Christ's second coming. To suppose that believers receive their immortal bodies while their mortal bodies are in the grave is to suppose that the resurrection has already come. Paul characterizes all such speculations as "godless chatter." He identified Hymenaeus and Philetus as two men who "wandered away from the truth" and destroyed the faith of others by teaching that the resurrection had "already taken place" (2 Timothy 2:16, 18).

Finally, our eternal bodies are numerically identical to the bodies we now possess. As Christ rose in the same physical body in which he died, so too we will be raised in the same physical body in which we die. In other words, our resurrection body is not a second temporary body; rather, it is our present body transformed (1 Corinthians 15:42–43). While a biblical perspective does not dictate that every cell of our present body be restored in the resurrection, it does require continuity between the body that is and the body that will be.

One day, the very body of my father that I watched being lowered into the ground will rise from its grave. It was sown a perishable body, it will be raised imperishable; it was sown in dishonor, it will be raised in glory; it was sown in weakness, it will be raised in power; it was sown a natural body, it is raised a spiritual body (1 Corinthians 15:42–44). On that day, my dad will no longer have a body dominated by natural proclivities; instead, he will have a supernatural, spiritual body dominated by the Holy Spirit and set free from slavery to sin—"an eternal house in heaven, not built by human hands" (2 Corinthians 5:1). Apart from that hope, there is no hope. "If the dead are not raised," says Paul, "'let us eat and drink, for tomorrow we die'" (1 Corinthians 15:32).

In short, Scripture describes the moment of death as disembodiment, not re-embodiment. Paul makes it clear that being at home with the Lord is tantamount to being "away from the body." If believers receive their resurrected bodies at the moment of death, they obviously could not receive them at the second coming of Christ, as Scripture teaches. Moreover, there is one-to-one correspondence between the body when it dies and the body when it rises. Thus, our resurrection bodies are not second bodies but our present bodies transformed.

WHAT WILL OUR RESURRECTED BODIES BE LIKE?

No more bulging middles or balding tops. No varicose veins or crow's-feet. No more cellulite or support hose. Forget the thunder thighs and highway hips. Just a quick leap-frog over the tombstone, and it's the body you've always dreamed of. Fit and trim, smooth and sleek.

—JONI EARECKSON TADA

Ever wonder what your resurrected body will be like? Hindus don't. Deeds in previous lives determine whether a Hindu is reincarnated as a monkey or mosquito, a walrus or wasp. In like fashion Buddhists hope to erase karmic debt and achieve the nirvanic realization of *no self*—to be liberated from an endless cycle of death and reincarnation (*samsara*). In other words, they hope to be liberated from the body. And if you asked a philosophical naturalist what a glorified body might be like, the response would likely be, "What body?" Only in Christianity is the question of a glorified body relevant. The Christian response may be summed up in three words: *Savior, seed,* and *Spirit-dominated.*

First, of all that can be said concerning our glorified bodies, the foremost is this: our lowly bodies will be transformed. How? Our *Savior* will "transform our lowly bodies, so that they will be like his glorious body" (Philippians 3:21). Like our Savior's body, our resurrection body will be a real, physical, flesh-and-bone body perfectly engineered for "a new heaven and a new earth" (Revelation 21:1). As we have seen, just as there is a one-to-one correspondence between the body of Christ that died and the body that rose, so too our resurrection bodies will be numerically identical to the bodies we now possess. In other words, our resurrection bodies are not second bodies; rather, they are our present bodies transformed.

Furthermore, we should note that the *seed* for our glorified body is in the body we now possess. The apostle Paul provides us with a seed analogy (1 Corinthians 15:35–38). As a seed is transformed into the body it will be, so too our mortal body will be transformed into the immortal body it will be. Hence, the blueprint for the glorified body is in the body we now possess. As a common caterpillar could not imagine becoming a beautiful butterfly, so too it is impossible for us to imagine what will emerge from the blueprint. One thing is certain: the blueprint will pale by comparison to the building.

Finally, the apostle to the Gentiles wants us to know that the natural body will be raised a spiritual body—that is, a body that is *Spirit-dominated.* When Paul employs the term "spiritual body" (1 Corinthians 15:44), he is not communicating that we will be resurrected as spirit beings but that our resurrected bodies will be *supernatural, sin-free,* and *Spirit-dominated*—dominated by the Holy Spirit rather than dominated by hedonistic sensations or natural proclivities. In place of "sexual immorality, impurity and debauchery; idolatry and witchcraft; hatred, discord, jealousy, fits of rage, selfish ambition, dissensions, factions and envy; drunkenness, orgies, and the like" (Galatians 5:19–21), we will faithfully manifest the fruit of the Spirit, which is "love, joy, peace, patience, kindness, goodness, faithfulness, gentleness and self-control" (vv. 22–23).

When we receive our spiritual bodies, what we are now in position only we will then be in practice. In the meantime, we eagerly await the metamorphosis that will transform our natural bodies into bodies that are supernatural, sin-free, and Spirit-dominated.

WILL EARTH BE RESURRECTED?

God is rich in all things, and everything is his. It is therefore fitting that the creation itself, having been restored to its primeval condition, should without restraint be under the dominion of the righteous.

—IRENAEUS

When the apostle Peter wrote, "We are looking forward to a new heaven and a new earth, the home of righteousness" (2 Peter 3:13), he was not describing an earth altogether different from the one we now inhabit but rather the cosmos resurrected without decay, disease, destruction, or death.

First, we might rightly conclude that the cosmos will be resurrected, not annihilated, on the basis of Christ's conquest over Satan. As the cross ultimately liberates us from death and disease, so too it will liberate the cosmos from destruction and decay (Romans 8:20–21).

Furthermore, the Greek word used to designate the newness of the cosmos is *kainos*, meaning "new in quality," not in kind—a cosmos existing in continuity with the present creation. Put another way, the earth will be thoroughly transformed, not totally terminated. When a flood destroys an island, it does not cease to exist, nor will the earth when it is renewed by fire.

Finally, the metaphor of childbirth is instructive: from paradise lost will emerge paradise restored. As Scripture puts it, "The whole creation has been groaning as in the pains of *childbirth* right up to the present time" (Romans 8:22). But, like a mother, earth will birth a new Eden in which God will wipe every tear from our eyes (Revelation 21:1–4).

CHAPTER
TWO

⋮

What happens to us in heaven?

IF HEAVEN IS PERFECT, WON'T IT BE PERFECTLY BORING?

Mystery is our mind's food. If we truly said, "I have seen everything," we would conclude, as did the author of Ecclesiastes, "all is vanity."
—PETER KREEFT

A prevalent perception in Christianity and the culture is that heaven is going to be one big bore. Pardon the analogy, but a never-ending repetition of holes-in-one would make even Tiger Woods want to give up the game of golf. That, however, is far from what heaven will be. Heaven will be a place of continuous new horizons, constant growth, and incomprehensible development. By nature, humans are finite, and that is how it always will be. Thus, while we will have an incredible capacity to learn, we will never come to the end of learning. So will heaven be boring? Not on your life!

First, finite creations will never come to the end of exploring the infinite Creator. What we now merely apprehend about our Savior, we will spend an eternity seeking to comprehend. Imagine finally beginning to get a handle on how God is one in nature and three in person. Imagine exploring the depths of God's love, wisdom, and holiness. Imagine forever growing in our capacities to fathom his immensity, immutability, and incomprehensibility. And to top it off, the more we come to know him, the more there will be to know.

Knowing God is an incomparable good. There is nothing greater. Indeed, knowing God is the essence of excitement, the antithesis of boredom. I fear that those who suppose heaven will be boring are like children addicted to virtual reality while all around them there is a world full of realism and relationships left begging to be explored. During his earthly sojourn Jesus often withdrew to lonely places and prayed. Why? Because he treasured fellowship with his heavenly Father. How much more should finite humanity treasure the thought of forever growing in relationship with the One who created us for eternal love and togetherness?

Furthermore, as we will never come to the end of exploring our Creator, so too we will never come to an end of exploring fellow sojourners robed in celestial glory. Indeed, our ability to appreciate one another will be enhanced exponentially in glory. Imagine being able to love another human being without even a tinge of selfishness. Imagine appreciating—no, *reveling*—in the exalted capacities and station that God bestows on another without so much as a modicum of jealousy.

Imagine the greatest, deepest, and most fulfilling relationship you have ever experienced on earth. By comparison to what you will experience in heaven it is but a shadow. No selfishness to clutter the canvas. No self-righteousness to fray the edges. No sin to blotch the portrait. In heaven relationships will be just that, relationships. The deep, rich, rewarding, wonderful intersection of lives on a never-ending quest from glory to glory.

Finally, we will never ever come to an end of exploring the Creator's creative handiwork. The universe will literally be our playground. Even if we were capable of exhausting the "new heaven and new earth" (Revelation 21:1), God could create new vistas for us to explore. Every faculty will be gloriously engaged; every sensation optimized. As A. A. Hodge, first president of Princeton seminary, well said, in our eternal home we will experience "the exercise of all the faculties, the gratification of all tastes, the development of all talent capacities, the realization of all ideals. The reason, the intellectual curiosity, the imagination, the aesthetic instincts, the holy affections, the social affinities, the inexhaustible resources of strength and power native to the human soul must all find in heaven exercise and satisfaction."[1]

So will heaven be perfect? Absolutely! Will it be boring? Absolutely not! We will learn without error—but make no mistake, we *will* learn; we will grow; and we *will* develop. Far from being dead and dull, heaven will be an exhilarating, exciting experience that will never come to an end.

WILL WE REMEMBER OUR EARTHLY JOYS AND SORROWS IN HEAVEN?

The positions of authority and the treasures we're granted in Heaven will perpetually remind us of our life on Earth, because what we do on Earth will earn us those rewards.

—RANDY ALCORN

It is not uncommon for Bible believers to suppose that in eternity they will have no remembrance of that which took place on earth. Indeed, God, through the prophet Isaiah, seems to say as much: "Behold, I will create new heavens and a new earth. The former things *will not be remembered*, nor will they come to mind" (65:17). Thus, on the basis of the Bible, we can safely conclude that we will *not* remember former friends and family, or for that matter, favorite foods and fancies. Or will we?

First, a text out of context is a pretext—which is clearly the case with respect to the above interpretation of Isaiah 65:17. In context, God makes a distinction between the judgment that will befall apostate Israel and the joy that awaits true Israel. In doing so, he makes clear that "the former things will not be remembered"; rather, "the past troubles will be forgotten and hidden from *my* eyes" (v. 16). The point, of course, is not to suggest that God is forgetful or that he has physical eyes. Rather in redemption, God does not remember our sins against us—he does not so much as "see" them anymore.

Furthermore, we too will no longer remember the former things, nor will they ever come to mind; for in the new heaven and the new earth, there will be "no more death or mourning or crying or pain, for the old order of things has passed away. He who was seated on the throne said, I am making everything new" (Revelation 21:4–5). The point here is not that we will have no recollection of life on earth but that the joy of heaven will be so great that our former trials, travails, and troubles will be eclipsed by a new order of things in which righteousness and justice forever prevail. No longer will unrecompensed evil exist. The blood of the martyrs (Revelation 6:10), like the blood of Abel (Genesis 4:10), cries out from the ground in anticipation of the day in which God's wrath against evil and evildoers find their ultimate resolution. "For it is written: 'It is mine to avenge; I will repay,' says the Lord" (Romans 12:19).

Finally, we can be assured that in heaven we will not know less—indeed, we will most certainly know more. We will not only remember family and friends, but our relationships will be better by far. As the apostle Paul explains, "Now we see but a poor reflection as in a mirror; then we shall see face to face. Now I know in part; then I shall know fully, even as I am fully known" (1 Corinthians 13:12). Moreover, we can be certain that there is continuity between our present selves and our future eternal selves. We will not be altogether other; rather, we will be resplendently restored and redeemed in resurrection. As such, we will ever remember the greatness of God's grace in redemption.

In heaven the scars adorning the Lord of glory will be an eternal reminder of the greatness of the salvation purchased by his passion. "This salvation, which was first announced by the Lord, was confirmed to us by those who heard him. God also testified to it by signs, wonders and various miracles, and gifts of the Holy Spirit distributed according to his will" (Hebrews 2:3–4).

HOW CAN WE ENJOY HEAVEN KNOWING UNSAVED LOVED ONES ARE IN HELL?

Nothing proves the man-made character of religion as obviously as the sick mind that designed hell, unless it is the sorely limited mind that has failed to describe heaven—except as a place of either worldly comfort, eternal tedium, or (as Tertullian thought) continual relish in the torture of others.

—CHRISTOPHER HITCHENS

The stark reality is this: according to Scripture, there are only two kinds of people—those who on bended knee confess Jesus as Lord; and those, unbowed, who experience eternal separation from God's grace and goodness. The sheer weight of this reality has caused Christians throughout the ages to anguish over the lot of unsaved loved ones. Indeed, how can we experience perfect joy in heaven while knowing that friends and family are in hell?

First, it is appropriate to acknowledge that there is no biblical warrant for believing that our memories will be "erased" in eternity. Therefore, we cannot rightly fall back on the unbiblical speculation that all memory of our life on earth—including loving relationships with the unsaved—will be forgotten in the new heaven and the new earth. Indeed, far from forgetting, martyrs in the presence of God are depicted as remembering their martyrdom as they cry out to God for justice (Revelation 6:9–11). Moreover, Jesus' glorified body forever bears the marks of crucifixion as an eternal reminder of the price that was paid to purchase salvation (Luke 24:39–40; John 20:20–29).

As noted previously, there are biblical passages that at first blush may appear to suggest that in eternity all memory of earth will be erased, but context inevitably precludes the pretext. Noteworthy among them is Isaiah 65:17: "Behold I will create new heavens and a new earth. The former things *will not be remembered*, nor will they come to mind." In context, here, Isaiah serves as the mouthpiece of the Lord. As such, the former things not remembered are "forgotten" by the Lord, nor are they ever again brought forward in *his* mind. God obviously does not have recollection lapses. The point, of course, is not that God is forgetful but rather in redemptive love no longer remembers our sins against us. In the words of the psalmist: "As far as the east is from the west, so far has he removed our transgressions from us" (Psalm 103:12).

Furthermore, it is crucial to recognize that the memories of our sinful and painful pasts and our awareness of the perfect justice of God respecting our loved ones will only serve to enhance our capacity for eternal enjoyment. How? In heaven we will see things from God's perspective. It is as though we will be in a courtroom with full awareness of the scenes that have played themselves out in the course of human history. And we will know with certainty that the Judge of heaven and earth has taken every converging factor into perfect consideration. We will know that we know that the judgments of God are altogether right and true—that they comport with perfect love and perfect justice.

In eternity we will likewise fully comprehend that all who are in hell are there because they spurned the relationship that could have been theirs. Those who willfully resist the will of God, who reject God's good intentions for creation, are therefore justly condemned. As New Testament scholar N. T. Wright has well said, "If there is no place in God's world of justice and mercy for someone who has systematically ordered their life so as to become an embodiment of injustice and malice, then there must come a point where—unless God is going to declare that human choices are just a game and didn't matter after all—God endorses the choices that his human creatures have made."[2]

Finally, the joy we will experience in heaven is not a fragile state of elation characterized by frivolity but a permanent and steadfast joy characterized by a foundation in ultimate truth and reality. In the presence of the glory of the one true God, all memories of temporal trial and all feelings of familial fidelity will pale in comparison with the greatness and majesty of the One we serve. Indeed, in eternity we will treasure the justice, the love, and the mercy of our great and glorious God. While we now view reality through the opaque lens of mortality, we will then see things as they really are (1 Corinthians 13:12).

All of this, of course, should motivate us to make a difference while there is yet time. In his providence God has ordained both the ends and the means. He has ordained those who take his sacred name upon their lips to be his ambassadors so that the gospel may go forth to the ends of the earth. Rather than despairing about our own future potential for joy, therefore, our compassion for unsaved loved ones should motivate us to preach the good news of salvation through Jesus Christ while there is yet time. Says Daniel, "Those who are wise will shine like the brightness of the heavens, and those who lead many to righteousness, like the stars for ever and ever" (Daniel 12:3). Or in the words of the Master himself, "The righteous will shine like the sun in the kingdom of their Father" (Matthew 13:43).

In sum, there is no warrant for supposing that memories of lost loved ones will be erased in eternity. However, in eternity we will see things as they really are; we will exult in the balance of God's perfect love and justice. In the meantime, we must ever take seriously our commission to be ambassadors for Christ, rather than secret agents who have never blown their cover before the unregenerate world. "We are therefore Christ's ambassadors, as though God were making his appeal through us" (2 Corinthians 5:20).

WILL WE BE ABLE TO SIN IN HEAVEN?

> *It is all of us that chooses; nothing is left over. Therefore there is nothing in us that opposes the choice; it is certain; it is wholly determined. But it is also wholly free because it is wholly self-determined. The whole self chooses, the divided will is healed.*
>
> —PETER KREEFT

To assert that we are not capable of sinning in heaven would seem to suggest that we will not have free will in heaven. Yet to claim that we *could* start sinning again in heaven raises the possibility of another fall—this time in paradise restored. How then can we be certain that the problem of sin is resolved in eternity?

First, we can be absolutely certain that we will not sin in heaven because of what the Scriptures teach. As the apostle Paul makes plain, we who have been crucified with Christ have likewise been "freed from sin" (Romans 6:7). In this life we are declared righteous in position before God. In the life *after* life-after-life we will be righteous in practice as well. Christ's ultimate purpose for his bride is "to present her to himself as a radiant church, without stain or wrinkle or any other blemish, but holy and blameless" (Ephesians 5:27).

Furthermore, while in the present we are bombarded by the temptations of the world, the flesh, and the devil, in paradise restored the problem of sin and Satan is forever resolved. "Nothing impure will ever enter it, nor will anyone who does what is shameful or deceitful, but only those whose names are written in the Lamb's book of life" (Revelation 21:27). As the apostle John goes on to say, there will no longer "be any curse. The throne of God and of the Lamb will be in the city, and his servants will serve him. They will see his face, and his name will be on their foreheads" (Revelation 22:4). These passages, together with the whole of Scripture, imply that in heaven we will not be tempted to sin externally by Satan or his minions, nor will we be tempted to sin internally by the natural sinful proclivities of the flesh. Temptation is enticement to sin. Where there is no temptation, there likewise will be no sin.

Finally, in heaven we will be actualized in righteousness. Free to be what God made us to be. Far from robbing us of freedom, such actualization is the quintessence of freedom. No longer will we struggle with a recalcitrant will. As our bodies will be every whit whole, so too our wills. We freely give up the freedom *to* sin in exchange for freedom *from* sin.

In his infinite wisdom, the Holy Spirit inspired the human authors of Scripture to illustrate this unwaveringly faithful relationship between the Lord Jesus and the church through the analogy of marriage. The truly faithful and devoted husband is not free to cheat on his wife. He simply cannot bring himself to cheat on her. His love for her renders such duplicity unthinkable. Do we consider such a husband to be less free than the one who is capable of unfaithfulness? Of course not! The faithful husband, unlike the unfaithful one, is truly free to experience the great joy and pleasure of uninhibited intimacy and union with his wife. G. K. Chesterton—the prince of paradox—aptly put it, "Keeping to one woman is a small price to pay for so much as seeing one woman. To complain that I could only be married once is like complaining that I have only been born once. It is incommensurate with the terrible excitement of which one is talking. It shows not an exaggerated sensibility to sex but a curious insensibility to it. A man is a fool who complains that he cannot enter Eden by five gates at once."[3]

Jesus Christ is the singularly sinless and freely faithful bridegroom of the church. Likewise, in heaven the church will be his "holy and blameless" bride. A bride freed forever from enslavement to sin. Freed to enter through the narrow gate. Freed to enjoy paradise restored.

CHAPTER
THREE

⋮

What is heaven like?

ARE THERE DEGREES OF REWARD IN HEAVEN?

I want to put to death every selfish motive and prideful pretense so that when the Lord's eyes scan my service, what I have built will stand the test. I want to be careful how I build, and realize that every smile, prayer, or ounce of muscle or money sacrificed is a golden girder, brick, or two-by-four. I want everything I do here to be an eternal investment, a way of building something bright and beautiful there. That's how much things down here count.

—JONI EARECKSON TADA

Degrees of reward in heaven are not often the subject of contemporary sermons. They were, however, a constant theme in the sermons of Christ. He explicitly points to degrees of reward that will be given for faithful service, self-sacrifice, and suffering. Indeed, the canon of Scripture is replete with references to rewards. While we are saved by God's grace through faith in Jesus Christ alone, what we do now counts for eternity.

First, it is significant to note that in his most famous sermon, Christ repeatedly referred to rewards. In concluding the Beatitudes he said, "Blessed are you when people insult you, persecute you and falsely say all kinds of evil against you because of me. Rejoice and be glad, because great is your reward in heaven" (Matthew 5:11–12). Christ continued his message by warning the crowd that if they did their acts of righteousness to be seen by men, they would not receive a reward in heaven (Matthew 6:1–6, 16–18). Jesus Christ's message is crystal clear. Rather than fixate on earthly vanities, such as the admiration of men, we ought to focus on eternal verities, such as the approval of the Master. He exhorted his followers to store up "treasures in heaven, where moth and rust do not destroy, and where thieves do not break in and steal" (Matthew 6:20).

Moreover, Jesus made essentially the same point in his parables. In the parable of the talents (Matthew 25:14–30), Jesus tells the story of a man who entrusted his property to his servants before going on a long journey. Each servant received an amount commensurate with his abilities. To one he gave five talents, to another two talents, and to a third he gave one. The servant who received five talents doubled his money, as did the servant who had received two. The last servant, however, showed gross negligence and buried his master's money in the ground. When the master returned, he rewarded the faithful servants with the words, "Well done, good and faithful servant! You have been faithful with a few things; I will put you in charge of many things. Come and share your master's happiness!" The unfaithful servant not only forfeited his reward but was thrown into outer darkness, "where there will be weeping and gnashing of teeth."

Furthermore, the canon of Scripture communicates degrees of reward in the resurrection. The basis of our salvation is the finished work of Christ, but Christians can erect a building of rewards upon that foundation. As Paul puts it, "no one can lay any foundation other than the one already laid, which is Jesus Christ. If any man builds on this foundation using gold, silver, costly stones, wood, hay or straw, his work will be shown for what it is, because the Day will bring it to light. It will be revealed with fire, and the fire will test the quality of each man's work. If what he has built survives, he will receive his reward. If it is burned up, he will suffer loss; he himself will be saved, but only as one escaping through the flames" (1 Corinthians 3:11–15). Paul here illustrates the sober reality that some Christians will be resurrected with precious little to show for the time they spent on earth—they "will be saved, but only as one escaping through the flames." This conjures up images of people escaping burning buildings with little more than the charred clothes upon their backs. This will be the lot of even the most visible Christian leaders whose motives were selfish rather than selfless. Conversely, those who build selflessly upon the foundation of Christ using "gold, silver, costly stones" will receive enduring rewards.

Indeed, a selfless Christian layman who labors in virtual obscurity will hear the words he has longed for throughout his life: "Well done, good and faithful servant! You have been faithful with a few things; I will put you in charge of many things. Come and share your master's happiness!" (Matthew 25:21). While deeds are our duty, not the smallest act of kindness will go without its reward.

Finally, degrees of reward in eternity involve both enlarged responsibilities as well as enhanced spiritual capacities. An experience I had several years ago aptly underscores this biblical reality. I received an invitation to play Cypress Point, arguably the most spectacular golf course on earth. While the invitation to play Cypress Point was free, I have seldom worked harder to prepare for anything in my life. For months I beat my body into submission. I lifted weights, worked on stretching exercises, and pounded thousands of golf balls, all the while dreaming of the day I would experience walking the fairways of Cypress Point. Without my strenuous preparation I would have still experienced the same cliffside vistas and breathtaking views. I would still have been able to smell the fragrance of the Monterey cypresses and feel the refreshing sting of the salt air upon my face. All the hard work, however, added immeasurably to my experience.

That is how heaven will be. As a master musician can appreciate Mozart more than can an average music lover, so too my strenuous training allowed me to more fully appreciate the architectural nuances of Cypress Point. As phenomenal as Cypress Point is, it pales by comparison to what paradise restored will be. I spent one day at a golf haven; I will spend an eternity in God's heaven. It stands to reason, therefore, that I would put a lot more effort into preparing for an eternity in heaven with God than I did for playing eighteen holes of golf. That is precisely the point Paul is driving at in one of his letters to the Corinthians. Pressing the analogy of athletics he writes, "Do you not know that in a race all the runners run, but only one gets the prize? Run in such a way as to get the prize. Everyone who competes in the games goes into strict training.

They do it to get a crown that will not last; but we do it to get a crown that will last forever" (1 Corinthians 9:24–25). Thus, says Paul, "I do not run like a man running aimlessly; I do not fight like a man beating the air. No, I beat my body and make it my slave so that after I have preached to others, I myself will not be disqualified for the prize" (vv. 26–27).

WILL THERE BE SEX IN HEAVEN?

I think our present outlook might be like that of a small boy who, on being told that the sexual act was the highest bodily pleasure should immediately ask whether you ate chocolates at the same time. On receiving the answer no, he might regard absence of chocolates as the chief characteristic of sexuality. In vain you would tell him that the reason why lovers in their carnal raptures don't bother about chocolates is that they have something better to think of. The boy knows chocolate: he does not know the positive thing that excludes it. We are in the same position. We know the sexual life; we do not know, except in glimpses, the other thing which, in heaven, will leave no room for it. Hence, where fullness awaits us we anticipate fasting.

—C. S. LEWIS

What do you see in your mind's eye when the word *sex* is mentioned? A sultry celebrity? A blockbuster movie? A risqué magazine? Or does your mind immediately flash from sex to Scripture? Trust me! When it comes to sex, *Playboy* cannot hold a candle to Scripture. If you think that's an overstatement, just read a few pages of Solomon's Song of Songs. Tragically, what the Creator purposed to be pristine and pure, the creation has prostituted and perverted. But that is not where the story ends! God does not arbitrarily remove things; he redeems them. So will there be sex in the resurrection? Yes and no—it all depends on what you mean by sex.

First, we are sexual beings by nature or *essence*. Consequently, sex is not just something you do. Sex is what you are! Thus, the foremost reason we can say with certainty that sex will exist in eternity is that sex is not merely a word that describes an erotic experience; it is what we are by essence. In the beginning God created us male and female (Genesis 1:27) and that is likely how it always will be.

Furthermore, we can safely surmise that there will be sexuality in heaven because heaven will personify *enjoyment*. Men and women will enjoy each another—not in a merely physical sense but in a metaphysical sense. This reality is virtually impossible for a crass materialist to grasp. The materialist views sexual pleasure as a function of fitting body parts together. Christians, however, see humanity as a psychosomatic unity of body and soul. Thus, we are not solely sexual somas (bodies), but we are sexual souls as well. In heaven, the pleasure that the male and female sexes will experience in one another will be infinitely magnified because in eternity our earthly conception of sex will have been eclipsed. In place of selfishness, we will take pleasure in selflessness. Thus, we can rest assured that our temporary earthly passions are but a pale shadow of the pleasure we will experience in heaven when symbol is supplanted by substance.

Finally, we can safely assume that there will be sex in eternity because God created sex in *Eden* before humanity's fall into a life of constant sin terminated by death. In Eden restored, God will not remove our sexual nature; he will redeem it. In heaven we will experience a kind of spiritual intercourse that eludes our grasp on earth. In paradise restored, romance subverted will become romance sublime. It will be agape driven rather than animal driven. In Eden restored, our sexual bodies and sexual souls will fly full and free, unfettered by the stain of selfishness and sin.

Will there be sex in the resurrection? Again, yes and no. Yes, there will be sexuality in heaven in that we will be in heaven—and we by our very nature are sexual beings. And no, there is no warrant for believing there will be sex in heaven in terms of the physical act.

WILL THERE BE ANIMALS AND PETS IN HEAVEN?

Who knows if the spirit of man rises upward and if the spirit of the animal goes down into the earth?

—SOLOMON

Talk about a question that stirs up emotion! The suggestion that there will not be pets in heaven has caused more than a few animal lovers to get downright squirrely. There is, however, no need to go nuts. While Scripture does not answer the question about pets in heaven conclusively, there is ample reason to think that animals will inhabit paradise restored.

First, animals populated the garden of Eden. Thus, there is a precedent for believing that animals will populate Eden restored, as well. Animals are among God's most creative creations. Thus, it would seem incredible that he would banish such wonders in paradise restored. Says philosopher Peter Kreeft, "How irrational is the prejudice that would allow plants (green fields and flowers) but not animals into Heaven!"[1]

Furthermore, while we cannot say for certain that the pets we enjoy today will be "resurrected" in eternity, I for one am not willing to preclude the possibility. Some of the keenest thinkers from Joni Eareckson Tada to Peter Kreeft to C. S. Lewis are not only convinced that animals in general, but pets in particular, will be restored in the new heavens and the new earth. If God resurrected our pets it would be in total keeping with his overwhelming grace and goodness.

Finally, the Scriptures from first to last suggest that animals have souls. Moses in Genesis and John in Revelation communicate that the Creator endowed animals with souls (Genesis 1:20; Revelation 8:9). However, because the soul of an animal is qualitatively different from the soul of a human, there is reasonable doubt that it can survive the death of its body.

One thing is certain: Scripture provides us with sufficient precedence for believing that animals will inhabit the new heaven and new earth. In the words of Isaiah, "The wolf will live with the lamb, the leopard will lie down with the goat, the calf and the lion and the yearling together; and a little child will lead them" (Isaiah 11:6–9).

HOW OLD WILL WE BE IN HEAVEN?

If on earth he healed the sicknesses of the flesh, and made the body whole, much more will he do this in the resurrection, so that the flesh shall rise perfect and entire.

—JUSTIN MARTYR

The question of age has haunted humanity throughout history. "If I had been helping the Almighty, I would have had him begin at the other end and start human beings with old age," quipped humorist Mark Twain. "Life would be infinitely happier if we could only be born at the age of eighty and gradually approach eighteen." Twain's humor hardly obscures the ragged edge of aging. Shakespeare candidly characterized old age as a "hideous winter." A cold, hard epoch in which the "body uglier grows" and "the mind cankers." Billy Graham was equally frank. "All my life I've been taught how to die," said the great evangelist, "but no one ever taught me how to grow old."[2]

Graham's sentiments strike a chord. Likewise, those of Twain and Shakespeare. As I move inexorably through the seventh decade of my life, I have become increasingly aware that growing old is not for the faint of heart. Solomon said it well, "The living know that they will die" (Ecclesiastes 9:5). But there is a fountain of youth! While Scripture does not directly tell us exactly how old we will be in the new heavens and the new earth, Scripture does provide us with glorious insights respecting the state of glorified humanity.

First, when God formed Adam and Eve in the garden of Eden, he created them in the prime of life and with apparent age (apparent age, *not* appearance of age—there is no warrant for supposing that the parents of humanity were created replete with calluses on their feet, belly buttons, or childhood memories). Additionally, Jesus died and was resurrected at the prime of physical development. Thus we are justified in believing that whether we die in infancy, in the prime of life, or in old age, we will be resurrected physically mature and perfect, as God originally intended.

Furthermore, our DNA is programmed in such a way that at a particular point we reach optimal development from a functional perspective. For the most part, it appears that we reach this stage somewhere in our twenties or thirties. Prior to this stage, the development of our bodies (anabolism) exceeds the devolution of our bodies (catabolism). From this point on, the rate of breakdown exceeds the rate of buildup, which eventually leads to physical death. All of this is to say that if the blueprint for our glorified bodies is in the DNA, then it would stand to reason that our bodies will be resurrected at the optimal stage of development determined by our DNA. Whether infant or infirm, we will be resurrected physically mature as God intended humanity to be.

Finally, of one thing we can be certain—in heaven, there will be no deformities. The body, tarnished by the fall, will be gloriously transformed. You will be the perfect you, and I will be the perfect me. The ancient apologist Justin Martyr said it well: "If on earth he healed the sicknesses of the flesh, and made the body whole, much more will he do this in the resurrection, so that the flesh shall rise perfect and entire." What all the kings' horses and all the kings' men could not do, the Almighty will do—put us together again. For in paradise restored "there will be no more death or mourning or crying or pain, for the old order of things has passed away" (Revelation 21:4). Partakers of eternity will forever "drink without cost from the spring of the water of life" (21:6). If you are searching for the fountain of youth—there it is!

WILL TIME EXIST IN ETERNITY?

When you don't ask me, I know what [time] is, but when you ask me, I don't know.

—Augustine

Will there be time in heaven? In times past those who pondered time in eternity more deeply have posited three possibilities: *eternal timelessness*, *eternal present*, and *endless time*.

First is the idea of *eternal timelessness*. This is an improbable notion in that physicality requires motion and motion requires time. Since the new heavens and the new earth are physical and we will be embodied, time is as inevitable as motion and change.

Furthermore, there is the notion of an *eternal present*. No past, no future, only an eternal now, stretched and perfected. Although there is much concerning the nature of time that is difficult to grasp (the puzzles and paradoxes of time have perplexed the greatest minds in history), the notion of an eternal present seems incoherent and unlikely. In practical reality, an eternal present seems little different from eternal timelessness—a distinction without a difference.

Finally, there is the notion of *endless time*. Endless time is analogous to time as we presently experience it. Moment by moment, event by event, the future greets us in the present and then retreats into the past. In the present we are yet captive to the "tyranny of the clock" (*chronos*). In eternity such will no longer be the case. *Kairos* (time relative to purpose) will no longer be sabotaged by *chronos*. In eternity we will never come to the end of time. Instead, we will ever learn and grow and develop without error as we explore our eternal Creator and his extravagant creation.

CHAPTER
FOUR

. . .

What's up with hell?

WHAT IS HELL?

If your God is loving one second and cruel the next,
if your God will punish people for all eternity for sins
    committed in a few short years,
no amount of clever marketing
or compelling language
or good music
or great coffee
will be able to disguise
that one, true, glaring, untenable, unacceptable, awful reality.

—ROB BELL

If ever there was a question in need of an unambiguous response, this is it. While cultists like the Jehovah's Witnesses continue to denounce hell as an error of apostate Christendom, Christian pastors have moved on. The vast majority prefer to dwell on more uplifting themes. Hell has all but disappeared from our pulpits and no one seems to have noticed.

For Rob Bell, author of the runaway best seller *Love Wins*, hell is a virtual nonissue. For all practical purposes, everyone ends up in heaven. Mormons agree. The world's vilest people make it into the *telestial heaven*; lukewarm Mormons, religious people, and those who accept the gospel in the spirit world generally enter the *terrestrial heaven*; and temple Mormons go to the *celestial heaven*. Hell is reserved for the devil, demons, and a small cadre of devilish souls (such as Judas) who qualify as the sons of perdition.

Our Lord had precisely the opposite perspective. He warned his hearers that the gate to hell is wide, the road leading to it broad, and "*many* enter through it." But "small is the gate and narrow the road that leads to life, and only a few find it" (Matthew 7:13–14). Far from marginalizing hell, Jesus graphically described it as a "fiery furnace, where there will be weeping and gnashing of teeth" (Matthew 13:42). While some have sought to make the Master's metaphors walk on all fours, in truth they reveal a far more ghastly reality.

First, from the biblical text we may rightly conclude that hell is *everlasting destruction*. "Those who do not know God and do not obey the gospel of our Lord Jesus," said Paul, "will be punished with *everlasting destruction*, and *shut out* from the presence of the Lord and from the majesty of his power" (2 Thessalonians 1:8–9). "Destruction" in this verse should not be confused with annihilation or extinction. What is in view is desolation—as when the Lord made the land of Israel a "desolate waste from the desert to Diblah" (Ezekiel 6:14). Though the land continued to exist, its fruitfulness was destroyed.

So it will be with the unrighteous. Their lot is everlasting destruction. Make no mistake. The plain meaning of *everlasting (aiōnios)* is to last forever—eternal duration, never ending. As our Lord promised the righteous "eternal [*aiōnios*] life" so too he prophesied the "eternal [*aiōnios*] punishment" of the unrighteous (Matthew 25:46). Thus, on the basis of our Lord's own testimony, we may rightly suppose that the duration of the destiny of the unrighteous is identical to the duration of the destiny of the righteous—each is said to be eternal. In sober reality, being "*shut out* from the presence of the Lord and from the majesty of his power" clearly underscores the reality of continued conscious existence.

Furthermore, hell is *eternal torment*. In the gospel of Luke, Jesus speaks of the "place of torment" experienced by a rich man. While in the flesh, he was "dressed in purple and fine linen and lived in luxury every day. At his gate was laid a beggar named Lazarus, covered with sores and longing to eat what fell from the rich man's table." Though it was in his power to do so, the rich man did not so much as feign the compassion of a dog. Then in a moment, there was a shocking reversal of fortunes. Lazarus died and "the angels carried him to Abraham's side. The rich man also died and was buried. In hell, where he was *in torment*, he looked up and saw Abraham far away, with Lazarus by his side." The very beggar once comforted by foraging animals was now comforted by

Father Abraham himself. Seeing the father of faith far off, "he called to him, 'Father Abraham, have pity on me and send Lazarus to dip the tip of his finger in water and cool my tongue, because I am in agony in this fire.' But Abraham replied, 'Son, remember that in your lifetime you received your good things, while Lazarus received bad things, but now he is comforted here and you are in agony'" (Luke 16:19–31).

As the parable progresses, Jesus unequivocally describes hell as a "place of torment." Torments that may never be marginalized as the *torture* of cartoons or Christian controversialists such as *New York Times* best-selling author Bill Wiese. When asked about his twenty-three minutes in hell, Wiese described it as a three-hundred-degree, zero-humidity inferno, located in the center of the earth where grotesque reptilian demons tortured the damned.[1]

This, however, is hardly true. Far from devils ruling over the damned, the Bible describes hell as being "prepared for the devil and his angels" (Matthew 25:41). Moreover, the flames of hell are far from literal. Martyrs experienced fire! They were dressed in tar jackets and lit ablaze. What they did not experience, however, was the horror of being perpetually unloved by the One in whose image they had been created. Imagine the torment of perpetual existence in the absence of love and a sense of relationship.

This is precisely what the torment of hell is. While Lazarus experiences familial tenderness in Abraham's bosom, the rich man experiences the fiery torment of being deeply alone. We are created for fellowship with God and with the crowning jewels of his creation. The torment of hell is deprivation of that very thing. No Lazarus to assuage the thirst. No balm in Gilead. The extremity of hell's torment is so great that, with Jeremiah, we are crushed by the horror of it and plead that our eyes may be turned into fountains of tears (Jeremiah 9:1). And we do all in our power to warn the impenitent "so that they will not also come to this place of torment" (Luke 16:27).

Finally, hell is the *erasure of the image of God* in fallen humanity.

While animals are among the greatest of God's creative achievements, only human beings are created in the image and likeness of God (Genesis 1:26–28). Even after Adam's fall into a life of perpetual sin terminated by death, he is yet described as bearing the image of God. Therefore, "whoever sheds the blood of man, by man shall his blood be shed; for in the image of God has God made man" (Genesis 9:6). Whatever else the fall may have done to the image of God, it most certainly was not erased.

Indeed, from the fall onward the goal of redemption has been the restoration of God's image in fallen humanity. Scripture elucidates the mystery of redeemed humanity "being transformed into his likeness with ever increasing glory, which comes from the Lord" (2 Corinthians 3:18). As we now bear "the likeness of the earthly man, so shall we bear the likeness of the man from heaven" (1 Corinthians 15:49). The promise is this: when Jesus appears a second time "we shall be like him" (1 John 3:3). Put another way, when Jesus comes to restore all things, paramount in that which is restored is the image of God in redeemed humanity—an image now marred in sin, but then magnified in salvation. We shall on that blessed day bear "the image of the invisible God, the firstborn over all creation" (Colossians 1:15).

The glorious reality of the imago Dei resplendently restored in the redeemed stands in sober contrast to the ghastly reality of the image of God removed from the reprobate. The image that was splintered in the fall will be shattered in the forever. While the redeemed are daily being transformed into the likeness of God with ever-increasing glory, the imago Dei is daily fading in those destined for darkness. The language of "everlasting destruction" evokes the horror of what it will be for the impenitent to everlastingly experience the erasure of the imago Dei. To be as it were "brute beasts, creatures of instinct, born only to be caught and destroyed" (2 Peter 2:12). To be "springs without water and mists driven by a storm." To be those for whom "blackest darkness is reserved" (v. 17). When the imago Dei is extinguished all that remains is "wickedness, evil, greed and depravity" (Romans 1:29). We consider the beastly Nero, the murderous Mao, or the despotic Stalin and think we have plumbed the depths of human depravity and debasement, yet they are but a glimpse of what will be when the flickering flame of imago Dei is extinguished and inexorable darkness ensues.[2]

In sum, hell is everlasting destruction, eternal torment, and the erasure of the imago Dei in fallen humanity. It is absence of the very thing for which we were created—loving relationships with God and fellow human beings. Precisely what was subverted by the fall.

WHERE IS HELL?

I am the way into the city of woe
I am the way to a forsaken people
I am the way into eternal sorrow
Sacred justice moved my architect
I was raised here by divine omnipotence,
Primordial love and ultimate intellect
Only those elements time cannot wear
Were made before me, and beyond time I stand.
Abandon all hope, ye who enter here.

—DANTE

Some time ago, the world's largest Christian television network (Trinity Broadcasting Network) reported that scientists had discovered hell in Siberia. According to the story, scientists drilled a hole nine miles into the earth's crust, shoved a microphone into the hole, and heard the voices of thousands—maybe millions—of tormented souls screaming out in agony. As incontrovertible evidence, TBN founders Paul and Jan Crouch cited major newspaper reports and a letter from a Scandinavian Christian.

As it turns out, the news reports cited by the Crouches were a mixture of tabloid journalism and urban legend. And the letter? A hoax concocted by a man named Age Rendalen bent on demonstrating just how easily Christians could be duped. When Rendalen heard the hell story on TBN, he decided to have a little fun at the expense of credulous Christians. So he wrote a letter to the Crouches, explaining that while initially he had laughed at their hell story, upon returning to Norway, he found the newspapers chock full of documentation on the "hell hole." As a result, tremendous fear took hold of him, and amid dreams and nightmares of hell, he surrendered his life to Christ.

Along with his letter, Rendalen provided the Crouches with his translation of an article from a large and reputable Scandinavian newspaper, which provided further details on the hell hole in Siberia. The Scandinavian news piece reported the appearance of a "fountainhead of luminous gas shooting up from the drill site—and out of the luminous gas, a brilliant being with bat wings appeared along with the words, *'I have conquered.'*" When contacted by a responsible radio broadcaster, Age Rendalen confessed that the whole lot of it was a fabrication. "Religion," said Rendalen, "is no excuse for being careless with the truth." He went on to share his disgust for Christian sophists who long ago traded truth for "a *National Enquirer* gospel of cheap sensationalism."[3]

While many years have passed since the Siberian-hell-hole story was proliferated by Christian news sources, speculation regarding the location of hell has hardly died down. Indeed, at least six major earthly regions are now depicted as gateways leading directly into the cauldrons of hell—among them a volcano in Iceland, a cave in the jungles of Central America, and a lake of fire in Africa. Others suppose that hell is not located on earth at all. Instead they suppose hell to be located in the interior of the sun. There, amid the outbursts of helium, scientists have discovered a million faces etched in the agony of unimaginable heat. Still others believe hell to be located in a black hole somewhere in the vast regions of outer space. All of which leads to the question, where is hell?

First, it is worth noting that millions suppose that there is no such thing as hell to begin with. In other words, in their view hell does not exist anywhere. Instead God simply annihilates those who do not receive his goodness and his grace. Jehovah's Witnesses go so far as to write off hell as an error of apostate Christendom. Seventh-day Adventists agree. In their view the doctrine of hell stands in direct contradiction to divine revelation. In recent years such sentiment has caught on with a vengeance. Notable evangelicals who supported annihilationism included longtime professor of systematic theology Clark Pinnock[4] and John Stott,[5] dubbed by *Time* magazine one of the hundred most influential people in the world.[6]

Pinnock characterized hell as "an outrageous doctrine" that "makes God into a bloodthirsty monster who maintains an everlasting Auschwitz for victims whom he does not even allow to die." As such, he uncharitably characterized Christians who hold to hell as sadistically "watching a cat trapped in a microwave oven squirming in agony and taking delight in it."[7] Dr. Millard Erickson's response is worthy of note: "If one is going to describe sending persons to endless punishment as 'cruelty and vindictiveness' and a God who would do so as 'more nearly like Satan than God,' and a 'bloodthirsty monster who maintains an everlasting Auschwitz' he had better be very certain he is correct. For if he is wrong, he is guilty of blasphemy. A wiser course of action would be restraint in one's statements just in case he might be wrong."[8] Demonstrating precisely such restraint, the venerable Dr. John Stott denied the existence of hell in hesitant fashion. Said Stott, "I do not dogmatize about the position to which I have come. I hold it tentatively."[9]

While I am sympathetic toward those who, like Stott, anguish over the anguish of hell, the alternative seems to me not only unbiblical but unthinkable. It would be a horrific evil to suppose that God would create people with freedom of choice and then annihilate them because of their choices. God is perfectly just, and those who spurn the grace that could be theirs will suffer exactly what they deserve. Indeed, we may rightly suppose that the hell of Hitler will be radically different from that of a garden-variety pagan. Annihilation does not come in degrees.

Furthermore, there are those who hold that hell is presently located in the center of the earth, the center of the sun, or perhaps in a black hole somewhere in outer regions of space. While the story that scientists discovered hell in Siberia was clearly based on sophistry and sensationalism, multitudes still seriously consider that an actual entrance to hell may as yet be discovered. This, however, is far from realistic. Instead, on the basis of Scripture we may say with certainty that hell, though a *profound reality* is not yet a *physical reality* (note carefully the words "not yet").

This is so, in that death is the separation of body and soul. Scripture refers to death as being "away from the body" (2 Corinthians 5:8). Only when Jesus appears a second time will the physical bodies of human beings be resurrected. Says Jesus, "Do not be amazed at this, for a time is coming when all who are in their graves will hear his voice and come out—those who have done good will rise to live, *and those who have done evil will rise to be condemned*" (John 5:28–29). In the meantime immaterial souls of the departed continue to have conscious existence either in the loving presence of the Almighty or separated from God's goodness and grace.

As we have seen, Jesus depicts this reality in a parable respecting a rich man and a beggar named Lazarus. Upon death the angels carried Lazarus to Abraham's bosom, whereas the rich man found himself in a "place of torment" (Luke 16:19–31). What is important to note here is, were we to ask *where* this "place of torment" was—whether in the center of the earth, in the center of the sun, or in a black hole somewhere—we would most assuredly reduce our Lord's words to an absurdity. It's precisely the type of absurdity imbued in the suggestion that from a volcano in Iceland, a lake of fire in Africa, or a hole in Siberia, one can hear the voices of millions of tormented souls screaming out in agony.

As previously explained, while departed souls have *awareness* they do not, however, have *whereness*—that is to say, they do not have extension in space. Thus, to ask where a soul is, is to make a category mistake. As the eminent exegete R. C. H. Lenski has well said, "All conceptions of time and space, succession and distance, must be removed for the other world. We know that they do not exist there. But our finite minds are inexorably fettered to these mundane concepts and are unable to think in terms of the supernatural world. Hence the Scriptures, even as Jesus here, condescend to us and use earthly terms to convey something of the heavenly realities to us. If Jesus should speak in the terms of that world, no human mind would understand a thing."[10]

Finally, while hell is not yet a physical reality, it will be so when Jesus appears a second time. Then the soul of the rich man, along with all who are in their graves, will return to resurrected bodies (John 5:29). Hence, we may say with certainty that just as the righteous will be resurrected in a universe liberated from bondage to decay, so too the unrighteous will once again inhabit physical space.

Where, we simply do not know. Just as we cannot say with certainty what our resurrected bodies will be like, so we cannot say what the resurrected universe will be. Again, think of the caterpillar. The chrysalis is its casket. There constituent parts devolve into a mysterious molecular soup. And then resurrection. Out of the chrysalis emerges a being that is altogether other—the same physically but radically different organizationally. The resurrected caterpillar emerges with wings that allow it to explore dimensions previously out of reach. Eyes that once only distinguished light from dark now experience dimensions of color and acuity. Once it merely lived to eat. In resurrection it indulges the nectar of a previously unimaginable new world. As we cannot imagine what our resurrected bodies will be, so too we cannot imagine what the restored universe will be like. As with our resurrected bodies, the restored universe will be the same physically but radically different organizationally.

Somewhere in that new space-time continuum hell will exist as a geographic reality. It may even be that in the new heavens and new earth, hell will exist in a dimension as out of reach as the realm to which Christ is now transcended. Of one thing we can be sure, however: the redeemed will never accidentally stray into hell's borders. For hell is not merely a physical location but a relational dislocation. And relational dislocation will never be the lot of those who have been redeemed.

ARE THERE REALLY FLAMES IN HELL?

A breath of relief is usually heard when someone declares, "Hell is a symbol for separation from God." To be separated from God for eternity is no great threat to the impenitent person. The ungodly want nothing more than to be separated from God. Their problem in hell will not be separation from God, it will be the presence of God that will torment them. In hell, God will be present in the fullness of His divine wrath. He will be there to exercise his just punishment of the damned. They will know him as an all-consuming fire.

—R. C. SPROUL

The question about whether the flames of hell are literal or metaphorical invokes strong opinions. Charles Haddon Spurgeon, rightly called the prince of preachers, was inclined toward answering the question literally. "Do not tell me that hell is metaphorical fire," he thundered. "Who cares for that? If a man were to threaten to give me a metaphorical blow on the head, I should care very little about it; he would be welcome to give me as many as he pleased." Spurgeon went on to contend that there was "real fire in hell, as truly as you now have a real body—a fire exactly like that which we have on earth in everything except this—that it will not consume, though it will torture you."[11] The venerable exegete R. C. H. Lenski was strongly persuaded in the opposite direction. "Do not ask what kind of fire caused the flame by which the rich man was anguished," wrote Lenski with a faint hint of sarcasm.

"Physical fire as we know it on earth does not determine anything about the fire and the burning which are constantly predicated of hell beyond its power to produce the intensest pain. That fire torments the devils who have no bodies, the spirits of the damned before they are reunited with their earthly bodies, and finally also their bodies. Is that not effect enough without prying into the nature of that fire?" As Lenski goes on to explain, Jesus spoke of incomprehensible things in comprehensible language. "It is the language of a parent to a child about things that are beyond the child's comprehension. The parent must either be silent or descend to one-syllable baby words."[12]

While both Spurgeon and Lenski are exemplary Christians, formidable intellects, and popular exegetes, they came to a completely different conclusion in this matter. Rather than decide who is right on the basis of a personality contest or in the court of public opinion, we would do well to "test everything" in light of the final court of arbitration and then "hold on to the good" (1 Thessalonians 5:21).

First, we should note that a metaphor is an implied comparison that identifies a word or a phrase with something it does not literally represent. Far from minimizing biblical truth, metaphors serve as magnifying glasses that identify truth we might otherwise miss. This identification creates a meaning that lies beyond a woodenly literal interpretation and thus requires an imaginative leap to grasp what is meant. When the Bible speaks of God's throne as "flaming with fire" and its wheels "all ablaze" (Daniel 7:9) we intuitively recognize that an implied comparison is in view. Likewise, when we read of the lamps of fire before God's throne, we apprehend that there is more going on than mere fire. Indeed, as the Apostle of the Apocalypse explains, the lamps of fire are "the seven spirits of God" (Revelation 4:5 RSV).

Furthermore, to suppose that a metaphorical interpretation of hell-fire somehow makes eternal separation from the grace and goodness of God something less formidable is to miss the point entirely. One can almost imagine the laughter that Sunday morning long ago in London's

Metropolitan Tabernacle when Spurgeon suggested that one may beat him with as many metaphorical blows as he pleased.[13] But upon sober reflection a graphic reality emerges. Metaphorical blows may not be physical but they are nonetheless painful. A metaphorical knife in the back does not draw blood but nonetheless produces an abiding emotional scar. Drowning in debt does not destroy one physically but does nonetheless produce deep psychological despair. In like fashion the fire of hell need not be physical to be devastatingly real. Jesus no doubt used the metaphor of fire to get through to an obstinate people more concerned with physical well-being than the eternal state of their souls. To be at enmity with a holy God—to experience not so much as a drop of water to assuage the thirst of such separation—is indeed a fearful thing.

Finally, there is ample biblical precedent for interpreting the fire of hell metaphorically. Consider the words of James, the half brother of Jesus, who described the human tongue as being set on fire by hell. "The tongue," said James, "is a fire, a world of evil among the parts of the body. It corrupts the whole person, sets the whole course of his life on fire, and is itself set on fire by hell" (James 3:6). James obviously does not intend us to suppose that the tongue, which is itself a metaphor for human language, is a literal fire that literally sets on fire "the whole course of one's life." Nor are human tongues (languages) literally "set on fire" by hell. Rather, just as James uses the language of fire as a metaphor for the destructive power of words, so too he uses the language of fire as a metaphor for the destructive nature of hell. Similarly, the Bible uses the metaphor of fire to describe godly jealousy (Deuteronomy 4:24), sexual lust (Proverbs 6:27), and unbridled passion (Hosea 7:6). Likewise, the Bible not only uses the metaphor of "darkness, where there will be weeping and gnashing of teeth" (Matthew 8:12) and blackest darkness (2 Peter 2:17; Jude 13) to describe hell, but uses the imagery of "gloomy dungeons" (2 Peter 2:4), a lake of burning sulfur (Revelation 20:10), and a lake of burning fire (Revelation 20:14) to describe the horror of eternal separation from the very One with whom we were designed for fellowship.

WHY SHOULD I BELIEVE IN HELL?

Let not anyone who thinks that fear of hell should be put out of the mind of unregenerate men ever suppose that he has the slightest understanding of what Jesus came into the world to say and do.

—J. GRESHAM MACHEN

The horrors of hell are such that they cause us instinctively to recoil in disbelief and doubt. Yet there are compelling reasons that should cause us to erase such doubt from our minds.

First, Christ, the Creator of the cosmos, clearly communicated hell's irrevocable reality. In the Sermon on the Mount alone, he explicitly warned his followers about the dangers of hell a half dozen or more times (Matthew 5:29–30). Using hyperbolic language, Jesus drove home hell's sober significance: "If your hand causes you to sin, cut it off. It is better for you to enter life maimed than with two hands to go into hell, where the fire never goes out. And if your foot causes you to sin, cut it off. It is better for you to enter life crippled than to have two feet and be thrown into hell. And if your eye causes you to sin, pluck it out. It is better for you to enter the kingdom of God with one eye than to have two eyes and be thrown into hell, where 'their worm does not die, and the fire is not quenched'" (Mark 9:43–48).

In the Olivet Discourse, Christ brought further sobriety to the subject by making plain that, as heaven is forever, so too hell will never end. To the righteous the King of glory will say, "Come, you who are blessed by my Father, take your inheritance, the kingdom prepared for you since the creation of the world." Conversely, to the unrighteous he will say, "Depart from me, you who are cursed, into the *eternal* fire prepared for the devil and his angels. . . . then they will go away to *eternal* punishment, but the righteous to *eternal* life" (Matthew 25:34–46).

To the biblical imagery of "blackest darkness" (2 Peter 2:17; Jude 13), "the lake of burning sulfur" (Revelation 20:10), and "the Valley of Ben Hinnom" where idolatrous Israelites offered up child sacrifices to the gods Molech and Baal (2 Chronicles 28:3, 33:6; Jeremiah 7:31–32, 19:2–6), Jesus adds the metaphor of a "fiery furnace where there will be weeping and gnashing of teeth" (Matthew 13:42). Thus, he magnifies the reality of an eternal existence devoid of happiness and joy.

Furthermore, the concept of choice demands we believe in hell. As author and apologist G. K. Chesterton has well said, "Hell is God's great compliment to the reality of human freedom and the dignity of human choice."[14] Without hell, there is no choice. And without choice, heaven would not be heaven; heaven would be hell. The righteous would inherit a counterfeit heaven, and the unrighteous would be incarcerated in heaven against their wills, which would be a torment worse than hell. Imagine spending a lifetime voluntarily distanced from God only to find yourself involuntarily dragged into his loving presence for all eternity. The alternative to hell is worse than hell itself.[15]

Without choice, love would be rendered meaningless. God is neither a cosmic rapist who forces his love on people, nor is he a cosmic puppeteer who forces people to love him. Instead, God, the personification of love, grants us the freedom to revel in his love or to loathe him. Such freedom provides a persuasive polemic for the existence of hell. If there is freedom then there must also be hell.

Finally, common sense dictates that there must be a hell. Without hell, the wrongs of Hitler's Holocaust will never be righted. Justice would be impugned if, after slaughtering six million Jews, Hitler merely died in the arms of his mistress with no eternal consequences. The ancients knew better than to think such a thing. Common sense convinced Abraham that the Judge of all the earth would do right (Genesis 18:25). Likewise, David knew that for a time it might seem as though the wicked prosper in spite of their deeds, but in the end justice would be served (Psalm 73).

Unfortunately, common sense has given way to credulity. Common-sense distinctions between good and evil have not merely been blurred; they have been obliterated. The Russian revolution foment-ed by Vladimir Lenin in 1917—a socialist revolution that led to the largest-scale massacre of a domestic society in human history—was romanticized in 1971 by John Lennon. The popular singer not only immortalized a secular humanist experiment that endeavored to establish a godless civilization but implored devotees to "imagine" reality without a heaven or hell. Ronald Reagan was far more real-istic: "Socialism only works in two places," he quipped, "heaven where they don't need it, and hell where they already have it."[16]

Common sense dictates that without hell there is no need for a Savior in this world or the next. Little needs to be said about the absur-dity of suggesting that the Creator should suffer more than the cumu-lative sufferings of all of humanity, if there is no hell to save us from. Without hell, there is no need for salvation. Without salvation, there is no need for sacrifice. And without sacrifice, there is no need for a Savior. As much as we may wish to think all will be saved, common sense pre-cludes that possibility.

In sum, Christ, choice, and common sense demand that there be an eternal hell. Far from rubbing out the crowning jewels of creation, Christ affords humanity the freedom to choose between redemption and rebellion. It would be a horrific evil to think that God would create human beings with freedom of choice and then capriciously annihilate some of them because of their choices.[17] Far be it from God! Will not the Judge of the entire earth do what is just? Those who spurn the grace that could have been theirs will be rewarded justly with what they deserve.

ARE THERE DEGREES OF PUNISHMENT IN HELL?

To some extent, the different degrees of punishment reflect the fact that hell is God's leaving sinful man with the particular character that he fashioned for himself in this life.

—MILLARD J. ERICKSON

On the basis of the Bible we may safely conclude that not all existence in hell is equal. Indeed, we may conclude that the torment of Hitler's hell will greatly exceed that experienced by a garden-variety pagan. As noted, God is perfectly just, and each person who spurns the grace that could be theirs will suffer exactly what they deserve.

First, the unified testimony of Scripture is that God is perfectly just and will reward and punish each person in accordance with what he or she has done (Psalm 62:12; Proverbs 24:12; Jeremiah 17:10; Ezekiel 18:20, 30; 1 Corinthians 3:8, 11–15; 2 Corinthians 5:10; Colossians 3:23–25; 1 Peter 1:17; Revelation 20:12). While a multitude of passages in Scripture demonstrate conclusively that there are degrees of reward in heaven and degrees of punishment in hell, the words of the apostle Paul in the book of Romans are particularly sobering: "But because of your stubborness and your unrepentant heart, you are storing up wrath against yourself for the day of God's wrath, when his righteous judgment will be revealed. God 'will give to each person according to what he has done.' To those who by persistence in doing good seek glory, honor, and immortality, he will give eternal life. But for those who are self-seeking and who reject the truth and follow evil, there will be wrath and anger" (2:5–8).

Furthermore, the Bible is clear that with greater revelation and responsibility comes stricter judgment (James 3:1). Jesus warned the Pharisees that they would "be punished most severely" for their willful hypocrisy (Luke 20:47). Denouncing the cities in which most of his miracles had been performed, Jesus said, "Woe to you, Korazin! Woe to you, Bethsaida! If the miracles that were performed in you had been performed in Tyre and Sidon, they would have repented long ago in sackcloth and ashes" (Matthew 11:21). Thus, said Jesus, "It will be more bearable for Tyre and Sidon on the day of judgment than for you" (v. 22). Moreover, Jesus used the metaphor of physical torture to warn his hearers that those who knowingly disobey will experience greater torment in hell than those who disobey in ignorance (Luke 12:47–48).

Finally, the canon of Scripture ratifies the commonsense notion that not all sins are created equal. Speaking of his betrayal by Judas, Jesus said to Pilate, "You would have no power over me if it were not given to you from above. Therefore the one who handed me over to you is guilty of a *greater sin*" (John 19:11). As Judas' sin was greater than that of Pilate, so it stands to reason that murdering someone created in the image of God is a far greater sin than thinking a murderous thought. Every sin is an act of rebellion against a holy God, but some sins carry far more serious consequences than others and thus receive a greater punishment in this life as well as in the next.

IS ANNIHILATIONISM TAUGHT IN THE BIBLE?

Death, the most terrifying of evils, is nothing to us, because as long as we exist death is not present, whereas when death is present we do not exist. It is nothing to those who live (since to them it does not exist) and it is nothing to those who have died (since they no longer exist).
—EPICURUS

Annihilationism is the view that no one suffers for eternity in hell. Indeed, according to annihilationism there is no hell. Rather, those who persist until death in their rejection of God's gracious gift of salvation are snuffed out of existence entirely. Just as universalism is the rage in liberal Christianity, so too annihilationism has gained momentum in conservative Christian circles. Even the venerable John Stott argued for annihilationism, citing, among other arguments, biblical passages that seem to suggest the fiery destruction of the wicked.[18] But is annihilationism taught in the Bible?

First, a God of love and justice does not arbitrarily annihilate the crowning jewels of his creation. Far from rubbing us out, he graciously provides us the freedom to choose between redemption and rebellion. As we have seen, it would be a horrific evil to think that God would create people with freedom of choice and then annihilate them because of their choices.

Furthermore, common sense inevitably leads to the conclusion that nonexistence is not better than existence, since nonexistence is nothing at all. Moreover, biblically speaking, not all hell is equal. We remember the ominous forewarnings of the Messiah as they ring back through the ages, "Woe to you, Korazin! Woe to you, Bethsaida! If the miracles that were performed in you had been performed in Tyre and Sidon, they would have repented long ago in sackcloth and ashes. But I tell you, it will be more bearable for Tyre and Sidon on the day of judgment than for you" (Matthew 11:21–22). Jesus uttered the selfsame sentiment with respect to Capernaum: "I tell you it will be more bearable for Sodom on the day of judgment than for you" (Matthew 11:24). If annihilationism were true, Christ's words would be reduced to an absurdity. Plainly put, there are no degrees of annihilationism. As stated previously, Hitler will continue to exist. And his torment will greatly exceed that of a garden-variety pagan. God is perfectly just, and each person who spurns his grace will suffer exactly what he deserves.

Finally, when understood in light of the rest of Scripture the language of "destruction" and "perishing" hardly supports annihilationism. In point of fact, it affirms eternal conscious existence. When Paul informs us that those who do not love God or live according to his precepts "will be punished with everlasting destruction and shut out from the presence of the Lord and from the majesty of his power" (2 Thessalonians 1:8–9), he hardly suggests annihilationism. To experience *everlasting* destruction is to experience everlasting separation from the love and grace of God. To leave no doubt, Paul equates everlasting destruction with being "shut out from the presence of the Lord." Jesus Christ, the ultimate authority, explicitly informs us that the wicked "will go away to eternal punishment, but the righteous to eternal life" (Matthew 25:46). Jesus contrasts the ghastly eternal punishment of the wicked with the glorious *eternal life* of the righteous.

Why would God raise the unrepentant from the dead (Daniel 12:2; John 5:28–29), only to snuff them out in the end? The alternative to annihilation is everlasting quarantine. And that is precisely what hell is.

PART TWO

⋮

Life after Life: The Transitional Heaven

In the early morning as I scanned the news, my eyes lit on an Associated Press article titled "Literati Gore Vidal Was a Celebrated Author, Playwright." Emphasis on the word *was*. The date following the dash on Vidal's tombstone is now forever fixed as 2012. The article by Hillel Italie notes that "along with such contemporaries as Norman Mailer and Truman Capote, Vidal was among the last generation of literary writers who were also genuine celebrities—regulars on talk shows and in gossip columns, personalities of such size and appeal that even those who hadn't read their books knew their names." Moreover, "he was widely admired as an independent thinker—in the tradition of Mark Twain and H. L. Mencken."[1]

Vidal was famous for the best-selling novels *Lincoln* and *Myra Breckenridge*, and infamous for mocking "religion and prudery." In the memoir *Palimpsest* Vidal downplayed his "more than 1,000 sexual encounters" as "nothing special compared to the pursuits of such peers as John F. Kennedy and Tennessee Williams." Italie notes that Vidal "was fond of drink and alleged that he had sampled every major drug, once. He never married, and for decades shared a scenic villa in Ravello, Italy, with companion Howard Austen."[2] Most noteworthy in Italie's article was the fact that Gore Vidal was quite certain that there is no existence beyond this life. "Because there is no cosmic point to the life that each of us perceives on this distant bit of dust at galaxy's edge," wrote Vidal, "all the more reason for us to maintain in proper balance what we have here. Because there is nothing else. No thing. This is it."[3]

But what if he was wrong? What if, after the worldly wise and wealthy Vidal died in the splendor of his estate in the Hollywood Hills near Los Angeles, California, he awoke in torment? If Gore is right, he is now merely cosmic dust in the wind. If God is right, he is now in much the same condition as the rich man described in Luke 16. Indeed, if Jesus Christ is correct, while the physical ashes of Vidal are being buried between literary heroes in a cemetery in Washington DC, the nonphysical aspect of his humanity continues to exist in anguish. While Gore Vidal dogmatically declared that there was "no point to the life each of us perceives on this distant bit of dust at galaxy's edge," he is dead wrong. Indeed, you and I are far from mere material beings living in a material world.

Reason requires those living in an age of scientific enlightenment to discard the "bit of dust" hypothesis. If we are merely material, freedom of the will is but an illusion. In that case, the vitriolic Vidal would have been fatalistically determined by his brain chemistry and genetics. His "1,000 sexual encounters" would not have been free demonstrations of love but fatalistic determinatives of luck. Worse yet, Vidal could not be held accountable in his eighties for what he did in his sixties and seventies, because from a purely physical perspective our body changes over time. Moreover, from the perspective of logic it is self-evident that Vidal's mind and brain were hardly identical in that they had distinctly different properties.[4] Of one thing we can be absolutely certain. While

Gore Vidal's physical brain is now dust in the wind, his mind continues in conscious awareness.

Post-enlightenment thinkers are, in essence, "wretched flatlanders." [5] Literati like Vidal, through might of pen, can transport readers to parallel universes, but when thinking about life after life, more often than not they retreat into fundamentalist paradigms. Instead of considering the possibility that they might step through the wardrobe into Narnia, they mindlessly mouth Carl Sagan's mantra: "the Cosmos is all that is or ever was or ever will be." [6] Far from independent thinking, they blindly suppose that nothing created everything, that life came from nonlife, and that the life that came from nonlife produced morals.

In life, Vidal vociferously contended that "there should be a constitutional amendment making it impossible for anyone to be President who believes in an afterlife." [7] In life after life, he might well, to borrow an analogy from the gospel of Luke, be begging Abraham to send Lazarus back to "warn" friends and family "so that they will not also come to this place of torment" (16:28). Make no mistake. The transitional heaven may not be physical, but it is nonetheless as real as the very flesh upon your bones. As we have seen elsewhere, whereas souls do not have *whereness* they most certainly do have *awareness*.

Of course, a great deal of misconception continues to surround the notion of life after life. Those like Vidal, or for that matter, like my father who died a decade and a half ago, do not presently experience the eternal state. That will take place only when Jesus appears a second time. As made clear in part 1, it is then that the physical bodies of my dad, Vidal, and everyone else who has ever lived will be resurrected either to a restored universe or to eternal separation from the One who created them for eternal fellowship. For now, however, Vidal experiences separation of the physical and nonphysical aspects of his humanity. Conversely, those who repent and receive Christ experience such brilliance and bliss that Paul goes so far as to say that "to depart and be with Christ" is "better by far" (Philippians 1:23). In other words, as wonderful as life is in the best of times, life after life in the transitional heaven while awaiting resurrection is infinitely better still.

There is much we can learn about the transitional heaven. In part 2, I address a host of questions regarding what happens in the life after this life, which we experience prior to the physical resurrection of our bodies. Not only so, I dispel a host of misconceptions. Is there such a thing as limbo or purgatory? What about ghosts? Can those who have departed return to this space-time continuum? Do those who have gone on before know what is presently taking place on earth? And is there any biblical basis for the concept of soul sleep? I also address the hugely popular phenomenon of near-death experiences. What are they? Do they provide accurate information on what unbelievers like Vidal or believers like my father now experience? What happens when subjective events like near-death experiences supplant the objective truths of sacred Scripture? And are purely naturalistic explanations sufficient to account for this phenomenon?

If you are a believer, it is my hope that reading through the entries of part 2 will equip you to think ever more Christianly about death and the afterlife. If you are not, it is my prayer that you will escape the company of flatlanders. The truth is, this physical universe does not exhaust reality.

CHAPTER
FIVE

⋮

What happens to us between death and heaven?

CAN WE BE CERTAIN THERE IS LIFE AFTER THIS LIFE?

When we die, we die—finally and completely forever. The idea we can somehow survive death is a myth.

—WILLIAM PROVINE

We live in an ironic age. On the one hand, it is an age of scientific credence; on the other, it is the age of Carl Sagan's creed. Philosophical naturalists, including atheists like William Provine, are convincing millions that we are merely material beings living in a material world. Metaphysical notions such as mind and soul are rejected *a priori*. Given the current climate, how does one convince a secularist that there is an immaterial aspect to our humanity that transcends the material and thus can continue to exist after the death of the body?

First, it is instructive to point materialists toward the reality of *libertarian freedom* (freedom of the will).[1] If human beings are merely material, libertarian freedom would not exist. Instead we would be fatalistically determined by factors such as brain chemistry and genetics. The implications of such a worldview are not merely academic. In a culture that embraces fatalistic determinism, we cannot be held morally accountable for our actions, since reward and punishment make sense only if we have the freedom to act or to act otherwise. In a merely material world, reason itself is reduced to a conditioned reflex. Moreover, the very concept of love is rendered meaningless. Rather than being an act of the will, love would be relegated to a robotic procedure fatalistically determined by physical processes.

Furthermore, *legally* (and intuitively) we recognize a *sameness of soul* that establishes personal identity over time. If we are merely material, we could not rightly be held accountable this decade for something we were involved in last decade. Why? Because our physical identity changes over time. Every day, we lose multiplied millions of microscopic particles in our body so that in seven years' time virtually every part of our physical anatomy has changed.[2] Thus, from a purely physical perspective, we become altogether other than we were. The reason a criminal attorney using this line of reasoning would not get very far is that as yet materialists function in a state of cognitive dissonance by intuitively recognizing our sameness of soul.

Finally, there is the matter of *logic*. We can prove that the mind is not identical to the brain by demonstrating that the mind and brain have different properties. The brain is physical, has extension in space, and is publicly accessible and objective. Mental states, however, are nonphysical, do not have extension in space, and are private and subjective. If I am daydreaming about donning a green jacket at the Masters, a neurosurgeon might well be able to observe synapses firing in my brain, but he could never observe the personal subjective images of my mind.

While arguments founded in libertarian freedom, legal sameness, and logic are powerful in and of themselves, an even more powerful and persuasive argument for life after life stems from the resurrection of Jesus Christ. As I argue in my book *Resurrection*, the best minds of ancient and modern times have demonstrated beyond any doubt that Christ's physical trauma was fatal, that his tomb was empty, and that his followers experienced Christ's tangible postresurrection appearances by which they were radically transformed.[3] Thus the resurrection of Jesus Christ provides the quintessential argument for life after life.

IS THE TRANSITIONAL HEAVEN A PHYSICAL PLACE?

Given the consistent physical descriptions of the intermediate Heaven and those who dwell there, it seems possible—though this is certainly debatable—that between our earthly life and our bodily resurrection, God may grant us some physical form that will allow us to function as

human beings while in that unnatural state "between bodies," awaiting
our resurrection.

—RANDY ALCORN

Many people believe that the transitional heaven is a physical place. After all, doesn't Revelation depict departed saints dressed in fine white linen robes? Are there not golden bowls full of incense there? And how about those golden lampstands? One Christian author goes so far as to point out that the transitional (intermediate) heaven must be physical because in Scripture the apostle John "is said to have grasped, held, eaten, and tasted things there," including a "little scroll" that "tasted as sweet as honey" (Revelation 10:10).[4] So of course the transitional heaven is a physical place, right?

First, we should note that, much like everyday language, the Bible is replete with figures of speech. Far from minimizing biblical truth, such figures of speech serve as magnifying glasses that identify truth we might otherwise miss. This identification creates a meaning that lies beyond a woodenly literal interpretation and thus requires an imaginative leap to grasp what is meant. For example, when Jesus said, "I am the bread of life" (John 6:48), he was obviously not saying that he was literally the "staff of life" (i.e., physical bread). Rather, he was metaphorically communicating that he is the "stuff of life" (i.e., the essence of true life). Thus, to "taste and see that the Lord is good" (Psalm 34:8) is hardly a cannibalistic admonition.

Furthermore, we should interpret Scripture in light of Scripture rather than embarking on subjective flights of fancy. Revelation is an apocalypse—not just in the sense of an unveiling but in the sense of a language system that is deeply embedded in the Old Testament canon. For example, Revelation is a virtual recapitulation of Ezekiel, from the four living creatures (Ezekiel 1; Revelation 4) to the eating of the scroll (Ezekiel 3; Revelation 10). Thus, when reading the passage in Revelation

10 about the apostle John eating the scroll, our minds immediately flash back to the prophet Ezekiel, who in Palestine (not paradise) is instructed by God to eat a scroll that "tasted as sweet as honey" (Ezekiel 3:3). As is obvious contextually, to feed on the Word is to "listen carefully and take to heart" all the words written in the scroll (v. 10). In other words, like Ezekiel, John is to internalize the words he is instructed to deliver. The words are bitter in that they portend the rebellion of those who bear the mark of the beast and sweet in that they signify the redemption of those who bear the mark of the Lamb.

Finally, it is crucial to recognize that God often communicates spiritual realities through means of earthy, empirically perceptible objects and events (e.g., the eating of scrolls that taste like honey), which, though unreal, provide us a means by which to ponder reality. Thus, when "the bride of Christ" (another metaphor) is given "fine linen bright and clean," this shouldn't for a moment be taken as proof positive that the transitional heaven is a material context in which a bride is dressed in physical clothing. Indeed, as the text itself makes plain, "fine linen stands for the righteous acts of the saints" (Revelation 19:8). Likewise, "the golden lampstands" represent "the seven churches" (1:11–12) and "the golden bowls full of incense" represent "the prayers of the saints" (5:8).

In sum, while the transitional heaven is nonphysical, it is nonetheless real. When Messiah said "God is spirit" (John 4:24) he did not for a moment undermine the Father's reality. Nor did Moses intend to underscore the Father's physicality when he spoke of the Lord God "walking in the garden." As God by nature is nonphysical, so the soul by nature is nonphysical. Thus, when Paul speaks of desiring to be "away from the body and at home with the Lord" (2 Corinthians 5:8) in the transitional heaven, he is invoking a relational rather than locational category.

Souls are spiritual and therefore do not have extension in space. Thus, to ask the location of a soul is to confuse categories. On the other hand, to speak of the soul being at home with the Lord is both correct and comforting.

DO WE RECEIVE TEMPORARY BODIES IN THIS TRANSITION?

> *We shall have to conclude that immediately after death we find our-*
> *selves out of our old body and in another kind of body. . . . The body*
> *experienced in this state seems to be an ethereal one, a mere shadow or*
> *prophetic hint of the more solid resurrection body we shall receive later,*
> *the Artist's preliminary sketch of His later masterpiece.*
>
> —PETER KREEFT

A common misconception in contemporary Christian circles is that upon death we receive a temporary (intermediate) body until our present bodies are raised at the second appearing of our Lord and Savior Jesus Christ. One author framed the argument as follows: When the apostle Paul "is longing to be with Christ (Philippians 1:21) he cannot long for a state of Platonic nakedness, which he considers repugnant." Thus, he would likely receive a temporary body in the transitional state until his present body was resurrected in the eternal state. Such is the case for martyrs in heaven who are "described as wearing clothes (Revelation 6:9–11). Disembodied spirits don't wear clothes."[5] Are such arguments valid or vacuous?

First, the notion of a temporary body is completely ad hoc. In the Philippians passage cited above, Paul does not so much as hint at the notion of a temporary body. Instead, in context, he explicitly contrasts being in the presence of the Lord with being in the body (1:24). To suggest that martyrs in heaven are wearing clothes (Revelation 6:9–11) therefore they must have been clothed with temporary bodies, of course, is to miss the majesty of metaphor. Those confused by the rhetoric may well find Revelation 19 helpful: "Fine linen *stands for* the righteous acts of the saints" (v. 8). And who can forget such poignant parallels in the Old Testament as "He has clothed me with garments of salvation and arrayed me in a robe of righteousness" (Isaiah 61:10)?

Furthermore, Scripture must always be interpreted in light of Scripture—the cloudy in light of the clear. To this end, we note that Paul in his second letter to the Corinthian Christians clearly communicates that the moment of death is one of *disembodiment* (away from the body) not of *re-embodiment*. It is not that he longs to be in "a state of Platonic nakedness" but that he yearns to be "at home with the Lord" (2 Corinthians 5:8). Moreover, the apostle Paul clearly contrasts our present mortal body with the promise of a resurrected body that will be immortal and imperishable (1 Corinthians 15). In making plain that there is continuity and correspondence between our present body and our resurrection body, he makes no allusion whatsoever to the reality of a temporary body that is altogether other than the one we now possess.

Finally, there is ample biblical evidence that the soul of a human being can continue to function apart from the body of a human being. Paul speaks of a man caught up to the third heaven (the dwelling place of God) yet readily admits that he does not know whether it was "in the body or apart from the body" (2 Corinthians 12:2–4). Obviously, if the soul cannot exist apart from the body, Paul would have had no reason to wonder at all. Moreover, we should note that as Jesus was breathing his last, he "called out with a loud voice, 'Father, into your hands I commit my spirit'" (Luke 23:46). And to the thief on the cross next to him Jesus said, "I tell you the truth, today you will be with me in paradise" (v. 43).

In sum, in the whole of Scripture there is nary a hint that we will receive a temporary body in the transitional heaven. Where the Bible does speak clearly the contrast is always between the mortal body in the present and the immortal body in the promise. And it is no problem biblically to conclude that the soul can have conscious awareness in the transitional heaven apart from the body. Indeed, it is a sameness of soul that establishes personal identity in time and in eternity.

IS SOUL SLEEP BIBLICAL?

> *Death is not complete annihilation; it is only a state of temporary uncon-*
> *sciousness while the person awaits the resurrection. The Bible repeatedly*
> *calls this intermediate state a sleep. . . . The soul has no conscious exis-*
> *tence apart from the body, and no scripture indicates that at death the*
> *soul survives as a conscious entity.*
>
> —MINISTERIAL ASSOCIATION, GENERAL CONFERENCE
> OF SEVENTH-DAY ADVENTISTS

Seventh-day Adventists are well known for promoting the idea of soul sleep. From their perspective, the soul of a man is indistinguishable from the whole of a man. Thus, the soul of man cannot continue to exist consciously apart from the body.[6] In making their case they lean heavily upon the book of Ecclesiastes—especially the words, "The living know that they will die, but *the dead know nothing*" (9:5). Such passages, however, must be interpreted in light of the whole of Scripture, especially the New Testament. The magnifying glass through which we read the Law and the Prophets must ever remain in the hands of the New Testament writers.

First, as the Bible makes clear, the soul is not the whole of a human being. The New Testament unambiguously communicates that the soul continues to have awareness though the body has died. As previously noted, in Luke 16, Jesus tells the parable of a rich man and a beggar who die physically yet experience conscious awareness in the intermediate state—a fact difficult to deny in that the rich man's brothers are living and final judgment has not yet occurred. Not only so, but the Bible's use of the word *hades*, without exception, refers to the transitional rather than the eternal state. Likewise, while being stoned in Acts 7, "Stephen prayed, 'Lord Jesus, receive my spirit.' Then he fell on his knees and cried out, 'Lord, do not hold this sin against them.' When he had said this, he fell asleep. And Saul was there giving approval to his death"

(Acts 7:59–8:1). It is clear that while the body of Stephen died, the nonphysical aspect of his humanity continued to exist.

Furthermore, as is obvious from the account of Stephen, sleep is a common biblical metaphor for death of the body—in distinction from the soul. John 11 provides the clearest of examples. Here Jesus tells his disciples, "'our friend Lazarus has fallen asleep but I am going there to wake him up.' His disciples replied, 'Lord, if he sleeps, he will get better.' Jesus had been speaking of his death, but his disciples thought he meant natural sleep. So then he told them plainly, 'Lazarus is dead'" (vv. 11–14). Similarly, in 1 Corinthians 15, the apostle Paul says, "Listen, I tell you a mystery: We will not all sleep, but we will all be changed—in a flash, in the twinkling of an eye, at the last trumpet. For the trumpet will sound, the dead will be raised imperishable, and we will be changed. For the perishable must clothe itself with the imperishable, and the mortal with immortality. When the perishable has been clothed with the imperishable, and the mortal with immortality, then the saying that is written will come true: 'Death has been swallowed up in victory'" (vv. 51–54). Here, as in myriad other examples (1 Kings 2:10, 11:43; Psalm 13:3; Daniel 12:2; 1 Corinthians 15:18, 20; Ephesians 5:14; 1 Thessalonians 4:13–15), the Bible speaks of the body asleep in death. Conversely, the Bible never speaks of the soul asleep in death.

Finally, if the soul did not continue in conscious awareness after the death of the body, it would be incongruent for the apostle Paul to desire to be away from the body in order to be at home with the Lord. Says Paul, "For to me, to live is Christ and to die is gain. If I am to go on living in the body, this will mean fruitful labor for me. Yet what shall I choose? I do not know! I am torn between the two: I desire to depart and be with Christ, which is better by far; but it is more necessary for you that I remain in the body" (Philippians 1:21–24). How could death be "better by far" than further fruitful ministry if it entails soul sleep? Paul iterates the same sentiment in a clarion call to the Corinthians: "We are always confident and know that as long as we are at home in the body we are away from the Lord. We live by faith, not by sight. We are confident, I say, and would prefer to be away from the body and at home with the Lord. So we make it our goal to please him, whether we are at home in the body or away from it. For we must all appear before the judgment seat of Christ, that each one may receive what is due him for the things done while in the body, whether good or bad" (2 Corinthians 5:6–10).

The point here, as elsewhere in the biblical text (Hebrews 12:23; Luke 23:42–43; especially Luke 23:46 in comparison with 24:37–39 and Acts 7:59; cf. 2 Corinthians 12:1–4), is that far from soul sleep, to be with Christ is soul satisfaction. While Ecclesiastes 9:5–6 is adduced to the contrary, Solomon does not conclude that "the dead know nothing" under the Son, but the dead know nothing "under the sun." When we die, "the dust returns to the ground it came from, and the spirit returns to God who gave it" (Ecclesiastes 12:7).

In short, soul sleep has nothing to commend it biblically. As the Bible makes clear, the soul continues to have consciousness apart from the body; sleep is a biblical metaphor for death; and conscious existence in the presence of the Lord during the intermediate state is something we may look forward to with eager anticipation.

CHAPTER
SIX

:

What is the transitional heaven like?

DO PEOPLE IN HEAVEN KNOW WHAT IS PRESENTLY HAPPENING ON EARTH?

Happiness in heaven is based on being with Christ, gaining accurate perspective, and living in a sinless environment. It is not based on a fundamental ignorance of what is happening on earth or even in hell.

—Randy Alcorn

This is one of the most frequently asked questions on the *Bible Answer Man* broadcast. People seem desperate to know whether or not loved ones in paradise know what is happening to the people on earth in the present. To rightly answer this question we must pay careful attention to the art and science of biblical interpretation.

First, many suppose that the departed know precisely what is presently happening on earth because the "souls" of the martyrs in heaven continuously cry out, "How long, Sovereign Lord, holy and true, until you judge the inhabitants of the earth and avenge our blood?" (Revelation 6:9–10). This, however, is far from a certain interpretation. During their earthly sojourn the martyrs had been instructed not to cry out for vengeance. Instead they were told to leave room for God's wrath: "For it is written: 'It is mine to avenge; I will repay,' says the Lord" (Romans 12:19). Therefore, the martyr Stephen did not cry out for vengeance but prayed instead, "Lord, do not hold this sin against them" (Acts 7:60). One can scarcely imagine the threshold of forgiveness being lowered in the transitional heaven. It is far more likely that, in parallel with the blood of Abel that cries out from the ground (Genesis 4:10), the blood of the martyrs metaphorically cries out in anticipation of the day of the Lord.

Furthermore, it is suggested that departed saints are even now watching and cheering us on from a great stadium in the sky since the writer of Hebrews tells us that "we are surrounded by such a great cloud of witnesses" (12:1). In context, however, "the great cloud of witnesses" referenced in Hebrews 12 is delineated in detail in Hebrews 11. From Abel to Samuel and the prophets they were "living by faith when they died" (11:13). Therefore, they everlastingly testify to the faithfulness of God, who in eternal promise "had planned something better for us" (v. 40). Nothing in the immediate or broader context suggests that they know what is presently happening on earth.

Finally, as has been aptly noted by Billy Graham, "The Bible does not tell us if the souls in God's presence know what is happening on earth. What it does tell us is that God knows what is happening in our lives." So "our desire as believers should not be to please men (Galatians 1:10), but to run the race to please God." Says Graham, "Jesus Christ watches our every move and knows our every thought. How thankful we should be, for He is our strength: 'The eyes of the Lord range throughout the earth to strengthen those whose hearts are fully committed to him' (2 Chronicles 16:9)."[1] The point is plain: apart from biblical precedence to the contrary, we should concern ourselves with the Lord—not loved ones—knowing what is presently happening on earth.

WILL WE BE LIKE GOD IN HEAVEN?

God wants us to become Himself (or Herself or Itself). We are growing toward godhood. God is the goal of evolution.

—M. Scott Peck

Our heavenly Father is omniscient, omnipotent, and omnipresent. The question is, will transformed humanity in heaven also be all-knowing, all-powerful, and simultaneously present to all of God's creative handiwork? The short answer is no!

First, we may be certain that even in eternity, saved humanity will never attain to the attribute of *omniscience*. Only God is all-knowing, and that is how it ever will be. Some suggest that since Peter underscored the great and precious promise that the faithful "participate in the divine nature" (2 Peter 1:4), they are indeed well along the path to omniscience. That, however, is far from true. Peter is not suggesting that we will be like God in his essence or nature; rather, he promises that through regeneration, sanctification, and ultimately glorification the saved are being progressively infused with the life of God.

The redeemed undergo a moral transformation of nature from that which emulates the corruption of creation to that which reflects the character of the Creator. We may rest assured that humans will never by nature be divine. Only God can carry the yoke of all-knowing here and in the hereafter. In heaven we will ever learn and grow and develop —yet without error. And mystery will forever feed the sunrise of each new horizon.

Furthermore, humanity cannot shoulder the millstone of *omnipotence*. Thus, in eternity we will yet be dependent on the Creator and sustainer of all things. Only God is almighty; only he is all-powerful. In the sound of a great multitude, in the roar of rushing waters, in loud peals of thunder, only he and he alone is rightly extolled as the "Lord God omnipotent!" (Revelation 19:6 KJV). Only he could create a universe in which the potential for sin is more regal than the lack thereof and still out of the actualization of that sin bring about the best of all possible universes—an existence in which we will forever be able not to sin.

God's omnipotence, of course, does not suppose that he can do all things. Thus, to ask if God can lie or create a stone so heavy that he cannot lift it is to ask a false question. Though God is all-powerful, he cannot act in discord with his own nature. God cannot lie (Hebrews 6:18), he cannot be tempted (James 1:13), and he cannot cease to exist (Psalm 102:25–27). Nor can he do that which is illogical. Just as it is impossible to make a one-sided triangle, so it is impossible to make a rock too heavy to be moved. What an all-powerful God can create he can obviously move. That God is omnipotent is self-evident truth. To think we may be omnipotent is self-deception.

Finally, humanity cannot attain to the incomprehensible sphere of *omnipresence*. Indeed, the danger of speaking of God in locational terms is that it implies God is by nature a material being. In reality, unlike human beings, who are limited by time and space, "God is spirit" (John 4:24). When Scripture speaks of God as omnipresent or present everywhere (Psalm 139:7–10), it does not suggest that he is physically distributed throughout the universe but that he is simultaneously present in all his fullness to every part of creation. As such, Scripture communicates God's creative and sustaining relationship to the cosmos rather than his physical location in the cosmos.

What God is in omniscience, omnipotence, and omnipresence we will never be. Even in eternity, we will learn and grow in knowledge—albeit without error; forever depend on the all-powerful, sustaining presence of the Almighty; and remain finite in time and space. As Solomon rightly proclaims of the eternal, ever-present I AM, "The heavens, even the highest heaven, cannot contain you" (1 Kings 8:27).

WHY DOES THE APOSTLES' CREED SAY THAT JESUS "ASCENDED INTO HEAVEN"?

Heaven relates to earth tangentially so that the one who is in heaven can be present simultaneously anywhere and everywhere on earth: the ascension therefore means that Jesus is available, accessible, without people having to travel to a particular spot on earth to find him.

—N. T. WRIGHT

Over the years, I have heard more than one skeptic ridicule the notion that Jesus ascended into heaven before the eyes of his disciples. In their view, even if Jesus were traveling at the speed of light he would not yet have escaped the confines of our universe. Not only that but he must surely be struggling with oxygen deprivation by now.

First, let me point out that to say Jesus ascended into heaven does not imply that he is *traveling* through space but rather that as the God-man he *transcended* time and space. In other words, there is no need to suppose that heaven is up there somewhere. As we have seen, heaven is not located in time and space; it is located in another dimension. As Dr. N. T. Wright well said, "Heaven and earth in biblical cosmology are not two different locations within the same continuum of space or matter. They are two different dimensions of God's good creation."[2]

Furthermore, the physical universe does not exhaust reality. It doesn't take a rocket scientist to understand that an effect such as the universe must have a cause greater than itself. This is self-evident not only to those who are philosophically sophisticated but to thinking people everywhere. As demonstrated throughout the history of philosophy (Aristotle, Augustine, Anselm, Aquinas, Anscombe), the cause of time, space, and matter is necessarily beyond the effect and is therefore timeless, changeless, immaterial, powerful, and arguably personal. As such, the notion that the uncaused first cause of the universe transcended the space-time continuum should pose no problem.

Finally, I should note that God often uses physical examples to point to spiritual realities. Thus, the physical fact of Christ's ascension points to the greater truth that he is now glorified in the presence of God and that our glorification is divinely guaranteed as well. Wright was right: "We post-Enlightenment Westerners are such wretched flat-landers. Although New Age thinkers, and indeed quite a lot of contemporary novelists, are quite capable of taking us into other parallel worlds, spaces and times, we retreat into our rationalistic closed-system universe as soon as we think about Jesus."[3] He is not presently somewhere near the outer fringes of our galaxy en route to a planet called heaven. Rather, having transcended time and space, he is as near to us as stepping through the wardrobe into Narnia. One step back through the wardrobe and he will appear again just as he ascended. In the prose of the Beloved Apostle, "continue in him, so that when he appears we may be confident and unashamed before him at his coming" (1 John 2:28).

In sum, while heaven and earth are as yet two separate dimensions of reality, when Jesus appears as he once ascended, heaven and earth will be as one. On that day the petition "your kingdom come, your will be done, *on earth as it is in heaven*" (Matthew 6:10 ESV) will have realized its resolution in reality.

CHAPTER
SEVEN

⋮

Are near-death experiences the real thing?

WHAT IS A NEAR-DEATH EXPERIENCE?

We rejoiced, and danced, as I was guided along this path to a great domed hall, that was intensely beautiful. It radiated with a pure, complete, and absolute love of God. And the beauty was such that I felt like I could see it and hear it and feel it and taste it all at the same time. I knew that this was where I and all people had a final opportunity to choose God or turn away.

—MARY NEAL

There is nothing new under the sun. During medieval times stories of predeath trips to heaven and hell were a potent means by which unbelievers were converted and believers convinced to remain on the straight and narrow path. Not until 1975, however, was the moniker *near-death experience* (NDE) coined by the occult parapsychologist and philosopher Raymond Moody in the runaway bestseller *Life after Life*.[1] But what exactly is involved in a near-death experience?

First, a near-death experience often involves what is described as an autoscopic episode during which someone views the physical world from outside their own body. For example, in *Embraced by the Light*, Mormon author Betty Eadie describes her spirit being drawn out through her chest and pulled upward, as if by a giant magnet. She soon found herself hovering near the ceiling looking down at her now-dead body. Eadie goes on to describe an out-of-body trip to her home where she watches her husband sit in his favorite armchair reading the newspaper and sees her children running up and down the stairs as well as engaging in a pillow fight.[2] After viewing various aspects of the physical world from an out-of-body perspective, roughly a third of NDErs promptly return to their bodies.[3]

Furthermore, in addition to the autoscopic experience, there are those who have what has been termed as a transcendental experience. They enter what is described as a dark tunnel, are pulled inexorably toward a distant light, enter a luminous environment, and encounter previously deceased loved ones as well as extraordinary beings of light variously identified as Abraham, Jesus, or Buddha. It was during this transcendental experience that orthopedic surgeon Mary Neal, in the wake of a drowning accident, felt her soul being pulled toward the entry of a "great and brilliant hall," in which the dead are given "a final opportunity to choose God or turn away—for eternity."[4] Likewise, it was during the transcendental phase of his out-of-body experience that three-year-old Colton Burpo encountered his mother's father, "Pop," adorned with a set of "really big wings."[5] In some cases, NDErs move seamlessly from the autoscopic to the transcendental phase of the out-of-body experience. In other cases they are said to skip the autoscopic phase altogether.[6]

Finally, a goodly number of NDErs report patently hellish episodes during their out-of-body experiences. In *Beyond Death's Door*, cardiologist Maurice Rawlings recounts the tale of a clinically dead woman floating out of her body, entering the obligatory tunnel, and emerging on a barren landscape crammed with nude zombies before gratefully snapping back into her body.[7] As a new Christian, I vividly remember sitting in church as my pastor recounted the hellish experience of another of Dr. Rawlings's patients who went into cardiac arrest while running on a treadmill. As Dr. Rawlings applied CPR, the man repeatedly reemerged from his hellish encounter in utter terror. It wasn't until the good doctor led his patient in the sinner's prayer that the man's condition finally stabilized. After working with literally hundreds of cancer patients, NDE specialist Charles Garfield documented a balance between hellish and heavenly experiences—some patients reportedly experiencing both.[8]

In short, a near-death experience is the subjective recollection of an experience that occurred during a state of unconsciousness precipitated by a medical crisis such as an accident, suicide attempt, or a cardiac arrest.[9] We should note, however, that the varied stories of NDErs are notoriously unreliable as a means by which to determine what awaits us when "the silver cord is severed" (Ecclesiastes 12:6). This is not only so because of the subjectivity of near-death experiences but because there is a substantial difference between clinical death and biological death (by definition, all near-death experiences occur prior to biological death). Put another way, to be almost-dead and to be absolutely dead are two entirely different propositions. In any case, to find out what happens after biological death, one is far better served to check the infallible repository of redemptive revelation—sacred Scripture.

DO NEAR-DEATH EXPERIENCES PROVIDE ACCURATE INFORMATION ON THE AFTERLIFE?

All I could think to ask was: "So what did the kids look like? What do people look like in heaven?"

"Everybody's got wings," Colton said.

Wings, huh?

"Did you have wings?" I asked.

"Yeah, but mine weren't very big." He looked a little grim when he said this.

"Okay, did you walk places or did you fly?"

"We flew. Well, all except for Jesus. He was the only one in heaven who didn't have wings. Jesus just went up and down like an elevator."

—TODD AND COLTON BURPO

This is an extraordinarily relevant question. In *Heaven Is for Real*, Wesleyan pastor Todd Burpo says that as a direct "eyewitness" his three-year-old son Colton was empowered to settle theological issues on death and the afterlife that the body of Christ has struggled with throughout church history. As a case in point, Pastor Burpo was unsure regarding the unborn going to heaven in that "the Bible is largely silent on this point." "But now," says Burpo, "we had an eyewitness."[10] Indeed, Colton not only settled the theological issue but was able to disclose such details as the height and hair color of his previously deceased older sister.[11] Moreover, says Pastor Burpo, Colton "had also been shown the future."[12] So Colton is now an authority in settling significant theological debates. Noted theologian R. C. Sproul, for example, believes the battle of Armageddon to be past.[13] Colton, however, knows—via direct inter-action with the resurrected Christ—that it is yet future.[14] Thus the question: are NDEs really an accurate means by which to ascertain information regarding the afterlife?

First, we should underscore that those who want reliable informa-tion regarding what happens in the afterlife are best served to consult the Bible. Also, on the whole we are far better served to pay atten-tion to teachers such as R. C. Sproul who have spent a lifetime seeking to master the art and science of biblical interpretation than we are to those relating subjective stories regarding out-of-body experiences. Two examples that stand in direct contradiction to one another immediately spring to mind—both involve Revelation 9.

On the one hand, Hal Lindsey, who has been described as "the best-known prophecy teacher in the world,"[15] says that "the *Spirit of God* gave me a special insight" regarding Revelation 9.[16] After much prayer, Lindsey was shown that the apostle John was "a first-century time traveler accelerated up to the beginning of the 21st century." There, he was "vividly shown all the phenomena of a global war fought with weapons of unimaginable power, speed and lethality." Subsequent to time-traveling back to the first century, John was "told to write an accurate eyewitness account of this terrifying future time."[17] Thus, the Apostle of the Apocalypse used first-century language to describe what he had witnessed in the twenty-first century: the "attack heli-copters" he saw he described as "locusts," the elaborate helmets worn by helicopter pilots as "crowns of gold," and the whirling propellers as "women's hair."[18] On the other hand, Pastor Burpo says that God likewise showed his son Colton the future. As a result, Pastor Burpo is not only certain that he will be alive at the time of Armageddon but that he will personally slay "monsters" with "either a sword or a bow and an arrow."[19]

And therein lies a significant conundrum. The Spirit of God revealed to Hal Lindsey that the locusts described in Revelation 9 are "attack helicopters" whereas the locusts were revealed to Colton as "monsters." Pastor Burpo is not subtle in chiding "theologians" who, like Lindsey, suppose the locusts to be "some kind of modern military machine." Says Burpo, "Maybe we sophisticated grown-ups have tried to make things more complicated than they are. Maybe we are too educated, too 'smart,' to name the creatures in the simple language of a child: monsters."[20]

What should not be missed here is that both Hal and Colton claim that their information came directly from God—yet their subjective experiences are in direct conflict with each other. If Hal is right, the locusts are attack helicopters. If Colton is correct, they are monsters. They can both be wrong. But they cannot both be right. Moreover, the code breaker for apocalyptic passages such as Revelation 9 does not reside in subjective flights of fancy but in examining Scripture in light of Scripture—what R. C. Sproul has rightly referred to as "the primary rule of hermeneutics."[21]

Furthermore, we should note that NDEs are hardly a way of ascertaining what happens after death in that a near-death experience and an actual death experience are two entirely different propositions. We may rightly suppose that what is experienced during clinical death and what will be experienced at the climax of death are not one and the same. The point here is that near-death experiences do not provide definitive knowledge regarding what happens after death in that NDErs by definition have not in actuality experienced biological death.

I should pause and note here that there are those who claim to have experienced far more than near-death. Pastor Don Piper, coauthor of *90 Minutes in Heaven*, may well be the supreme exemplar. "I died on January 18, 1989," says Pastor Piper. "Immediately after I died, I went straight to heaven."[22] If Pastor Piper is to be believed, he is singularly unique in human history. There are, of course, a handful of resurrections recorded in the Bible. None, however, apart from Christ himself, were permitted to record their experience in the text of sacred Scripture. This is so even respecting the great apostle Paul—author of two-thirds of the New Testament epistles. While he did, in fact, go to the third heaven, Paul did not so much as countenance writing a sixty-seventh book of the Bible titled *90 Minutes in Heaven*. Though he "was caught up to paradise" and "heard inexpressible things, things that man is not permitted to tell," he humbly refrained from boasting "so no one will think more of me than is warranted" and, says Paul, "to keep me from becoming conceited because of these surpassingly great revelations" (2 Corinthians 12:1–7).

In sharp distinction to the apostle Paul, Pastor Piper is more than willing to relate his surpassingly great experiences in person and in print. Indeed, he seems so convinced that he had *an actual death experience*, not a near-death experience, that he prophesied to a global Christian television audience that because he has already died—and people die only once—Jesus would return within his very own lifetime.[23] Even apart from date setting, what is particularly disturbing about Pastor Piper's testimony is the boast that he has been empowered to "speak authoritatively about heaven from firsthand knowledge."[24] This, of course, is no small thing. Prior to Piper, only the resurrected Savior has been able to do that. Indeed, among the biblical writers who "spoke from God as they were carried along by the Holy Spirit" (2 Peter 1:21) not one dared say that like his Lord he had been resurrected from the dead and could "speak authoritatively about heaven from firsthand knowledge." Nor did one of them dare prophesy the century of Christ's return.

Finally, one should be highly suspicious of near-death experiences in that celestial travelers return with wildly divergent accounts of the afterlife. Pastor Burpo writes that his son looked into the very face of God the Father and determined God's hair to be yellow and his eyes blue.[25] In sharp contrast, Alex Malarkey was permitted to see only up to the neck of God because anyone seeing the face of God would not have a near-death experience—but a now-death experience. Said Malarkey, "Nobody is allowed to see God's face or that person will die."[26] Likewise, Colton recognized "the clear greenish blue eyes" of the Jesus that he had seen in heaven after being shown a portrait painted by the famous child prodigy Akiane. "In Akiane's portrait," writes Pastor Burpo, we have finally "seen the face of Jesus."[27] Ironically, the face Akiane drew was that of a seven-foot man who unexpectedly dropped by her residence.[28] Thus, if the Burpos are right, their heavenly Jesus currently has an earthly double.

While Colton Burpo recognized Jesus from the model of an earthly man, Betty Eadie recognized Jesus from the preexistence she experienced prior to her birth on Planet Earth.[29] As a Mormon, Betty's perception of Jesus and his message is decidedly different from that of the Burpos'. For Eadie, Jesus is merely an elder brother who like other spirit children enter physical bodies for their turns upon earth, each experiencing the pains and joys that will ultimately help them in their progression toward becoming God. Indeed, in Mormonism, Jesus is merely a spirit brother of Lucifer who was conceived in heaven by a celestial Mother and came in flesh as the result of the Father having sex with the Virgin Mary.[30] Moreover, while Christians believe that God is spirit (John 4:24), Mormons hold that "God himself was once as we are now, and is an exalted man, and sits enthroned in yonder heavens!"[31] Mormonism also holds to a plurality of gods and contends that "as man is God once was; as God is, man may become."[32] It should also be noted that though neurosurgeon Eben Alexander "experienced a perfect storm of near-death experiences"[33]—an experience that allowed him to finally grasp "what religion was really all about"[34]—Jesus was entirely conspicuous by his absence.

All of this is noteworthy in that near-death experiences are predictably contextualized by the backgrounds and belief systems of those who experience them. As such, they hardly provide a unified conclusion regarding the matters of life and death, heaven and hell, and most importantly the nature of God. Christians who interpret the Bible literalistically are galvanized in the presupposition that God the Father has enormous wings and ever sits upon his golden throne. Kabbalists are solidified in their dreams regarding the transmigration of the soul. Hindus draw ever nearer to the impersonal cosmic consciousness of the universe. Muslims encounter the Holy Spirit as the archangel Gabriel. Buddhists are inexorably guided down the pathway to nirvanic realization of "no self."

This is not to say, however, that a good many NDErs do not go through spiritual transformation as a result of out-of-body episodes. Indeed, celestial travelers—whether via visions, dreams, or near-death experiences—are increasingly being converted to an intoxicating brand of mysticism that engulfs everyone in the bright white light of universal acceptance—and that irrespective of doctrine and deed. Indeed, Akiane and her family appear to have had just such a transformation. As a result of her visionary visits to heaven, Akiane, along with formerly atheist family members, began to traverse spiritual pathways ranging from Catholicism to Buddhism in a quest for spiritual enlightenment.[35] Though, in the words of Pastor Burpo, "her descriptions of heaven sounded remarkably like Colton's"[36] they have led her to an altogether different form of syncretistic spirituality. Suffice it to say Akiane's visits to heaven have not led to visions of family members slaying monsters in the battle of Armageddon "with either a sword or a bow and an arrow."[37]

Perhaps as disheartening as the spiritual syncretism that is increasingly popularized through near-death experiences is the selling and sensationalism surrounding them. As Elizabeth Hillstrom, professor of psychology at Wheaton, wisely warned in *Testing the Spirits*, "It is possible that some NDE accounts are grossly exaggerated or are even outright fabrications, concocted for profit, publicity or attention. Currently there is a very strong market for book-length accounts of NDEs, and unfortunately many readers are willing to accept such accounts at face value. This creates a situation that is ripe for exploitation by unscrupulous storytellers."[38]

Professor Hillstrom has hardly overstated the matter. In the last few years evangelical publishing houses alone have churned out one near-death story after the other. Just this morning I received another in a long string of such stories, titled *My Journey to Heaven: What I Saw and How It Changed My Life*, by Marvin J. Besteman. Ironically, in sharp contrast to Burpo, who gazed intently into the blue eyes of deity; and Malarkey, who under penalty of death was not permitted to see God's face; Besteman—who describes himself as not the kind "to put up with a lot of malarkey"[39]—saw a throne "about three quarters of a mile away" from where he stood outside the gate of heaven. It was adorned with "huge white pillars" and had "two Beings seated on it."[40] While Besteman, like Burpo, was permitted to see God, he saw him only from a distance in that he was resisted at "the monumental gate"[41] into heaven by an unkempt Peter replete with "scrubby beard, shaggy hair, and clothes that looked like he had been wearing them for 1,000 years."[42] Why? "Because when he opened the Book of Life for April 27 or 28, 2006 [the time of the quasi-near-death experience] the name Marv Besteman was nowhere to be found."[43]

Suffice it to say, near-death experiences do not provide accurate information on the afterlife. The best we can say assuredly is that they lend credence to the reality that the mind is not identical to the brain in that the mind and brain have different properties. But this we already ascertain from the infallible repository of redemptive revelation.

WHAT ARE THE LIABILITIES OF NEAR-DEATH EXPERIENCES?

NDErs manifest a deepening of intrinsic faith following their experience, but the direction that this deepened spirituality takes—that is, toward an Eastern religion, New Age spirituality, Christianity, and so on—appears to be influenced by factors other than the NDE itself.
—Dr. Michael Sabom

As documented earlier, popular interest in near-death experiences is at a fever pitch. From Raymond Moody's *Life after Life* to Todd Burpo's *Heaven Is for Real*, to Eben Alexander's *Proof of Heaven*, to Mary Neal's *To Heaven and Back*, NDEs have titillated the masses for the better part of a generation. New revelations ranging from the physical characteristics of the devil (three heads, earless, a nasty nose, and moldy teeth) and demons (green, long fingernails, hair made of fire), to descriptions of God the Father (blue eyes, yellow hair, and huge wings), God the Son (sea green-bluish eyes and a rainbow-colored horse), and God the Holy Spirit (bluish but hard to see), are captivating the minds of millions of evangelicals. The problem is there are significant liabilities associated with NDEs.

First, we should note that the substance of an NDE is inevitably informed by the worldview of the celestial traveler.[44] And that is precisely the problem. The objective reference point of sacred Scripture has been supplanted by the subjective experiences of those who have allegedly had a foretaste of heaven. Thus, while Scripture knows nothing of human preexistence, Betty Eadie—in concert with her Mormon presuppositions—alleges that while being embraced by the light she recognized the very Jesus that she had previously encountered in her preexistence.[45] In like fashion, Raymond Moody and Eben Alexander—in accord with their presuppositions—view life after life as devoid of the judgment of an altogether holy God.[46]

Furthermore, near-death experiences have been greatly biased by the subjective specter of hyperliteralism. It is not surprising that heavenly travelers return from the afterlife with stories of gates made of genuine pearl and streets manufactured from the purest of gold. Tragically, such exacting literalism is pandemic within the contemporary Christian community. Thus, it is not uncommon to see heaven described as a translucent cube measuring fifteen hundred miles in each direction. One writer goes so far as to calculate the city composed of pure gold as precisely 3,375,000,000 cubic miles fenced in by walls of diamond that are perched on 500-mile-wide foundation stones made of materials ranging from sapphire to sardonyx.[47] One wonders if, by the same token, the present earth is set on pillars. After all, does not the Bible say that God "shakes the earth from its place and makes its pillars tremble" (Job 9:6)? Small wonder that today's terrestrial travelers return from their near-death experiences with stories of massive pearly gates, brightly colored horses, and a Holy Spirit that is, well, "kind of blue."[48]

Finally, as I underscored earlier, there is the very real issue of apostolic authority. God himself set the conditions by which new revelations of life after life must be ratified—namely, confirmation by those who were eyewitnesses to the resurrection of Jesus Christ. In point of fact, with the death of the apostles there can be no new revelations—much less new revelations that compromise, confuse, or outright contradict "the faith that was once for all delivered to the saints" (Jude 3 ESV). Paul is the quintessential test case. The apostolic community validated him as an eyewitness to the resurrection and as an apostle. Thus, revelation received through him—unlike revelations received through modern revelators—may be deemed reliable and binding on the body of Christ.

I do not doubt that some of those who claim to have been to heaven (or hell) have had a subjective experience. But that is precisely the point. Subjective experiences are notoriously unreliable; thus, they must be tested in light of an objective frame of reference—which in Christianity is the Bible. Again, Colton Burpo may genuinely believe that God has yellow hair and big wings. But we do well to "test everything. Hold on to the good" (1 Thessalonians 5:21).

CAN NATURAL EXPLANATIONS ACCOUNT FOR NEAR-DEATH EXPERIENCES?

I stress that all NDE-related psychic phenomena can probably be explained through natural means. I would strongly disagree with anyone who claims that NDEs are inherently "of the devil." In my opinion, the NDE is a naturally occurring phenomenon. It can, however, depending on how it is responded to, bring people into contact with malevolent spiritual forces.

—RICHARD ABANES

Philosophical naturalists believe the cosmos is all that is or ever was or ever will be.[49] Therefore, they relegate near-death experiences to purely *psychopharmacological, physiological,* or *psychological* processes. This is precisely what neurosurgeon and ardent materialist Eben Alexander did. Prior to personally experiencing an NDE, Dr. Alexander simply could not reconcile his understanding of neuroscience with the notion of a soul that can exist wholly apart from body and brains. "The brain is the machine that produces consciousness in the first place," writes Alexander. "When the machine breaks down consciousness stops."[50] But "after seven days in a coma during which the human part of my brain, the neocortex, was inactivated, I experienced something so profound that it gave me a scientific reason to believe in consciousness after death."[51] Alexander's conversion was profound. "My experience showed me that the death of the body and the brain are not the end of consciousness, that human experience continues beyond the grave."[52] And herein lies a singularly significant question: are naturalistic explanations sufficient to account for near-death experiences?

First, there is no question in my mind that some near-death experiences are rightly attributed to the psychoactive drugs that are ingested during a medical crisis. Dr. Ronald Siegel, distinguished professor of psychopharmacology at UCLA, notes that Ketamine (a dissociative anesthetic that accelerates production of L-glutamate) can cause experiences strikingly similar to NDEs. Not only so, but through the use of peyote, a cactus extract that contains mescaline as the active hallucinogen, Indians in the High Sierra Madres, in Central Mexico—not exposed to modern cultural biases—have experienced episodes virtually identical to NDEs.[53]

Furthermore, physiological factors, such as oxygen abnormalities in the brain, may well play a role in near-death experiences. In her book *Dying to Live: Near-Death Experiences*, Dr. Susan Blackmore argues that oxygen deficiency in the brain can account for critical aspects of near-death experiences. According to Blackmore, the reality that such experiences can occur without anoxia does not negate the fact that a lack of oxygen in the brain can trigger both autoscopic and transcendental episodes in which NDErs leave their bodies and/or move through dark tunnels en route to being embraced by the light.[54] While perhaps not sufficient in and of itself, physiological factors, such as oxygen deprivation and the release of endorphins, may play a role in NDEs.

Finally, psychological factors, including fantasy proneness, may play a part in some near-death experiences. Statistically, one out of every twelve Americans is predisposed to creating a fantasy out of thin air—and then believing it to be true. Such fantasy proneness is referred to as Grade Five Syndrome.[55] While Grade Five personalities are generally intuitive and intelligent, they also have vivid, visual imaginations. Thus they are highly susceptible to the power of suggestion. A complex of characteristics, including the capacity to believe contradictory experiences, a propensity for the unusual, and an eagerness to trust and please others, makes Grade Five personalities particularly susceptible to NDEs, out-of-body experiences, and the occasional difficulty in distinguishing fantasy from reality.[56]

Considered collectively, *psychopharmacological*, *physiological*, and *psychological* explanations may well provide a compelling naturalistic rationale for the near-death experience. However, naturalistic explanations assume that consciousness is merely a function of the physical brain. In other words, philosophical naturalists, such as the aforementioned Dr. Siegel, are misguided in supposing that the mind and the brain are one and the same. We can be certain that this is not the case in that the mind and the brain have different properties. As aptly noted by Drs. Habermas and Moreland, "The subjective texture of our conscious mental experiences—the feeling of pain, the experience of sound, the awareness of color—is different from anything that is simply physical. If the world were only made of matter these subjective aspects of consciousness would not exist. But they do exist! So there must be more to the world than matter."[57] (This is something Dr. Alexander should have been well aware of even prior to his NDE.)

I would be remiss here if I did not underscore the horror of a purely naturalistic worldview. If we are merely material, libertarian freedom (freedom of the will) would not exist. Instead, we would be fatalistically relegated to a world in which everything is determined by mechanistic material processes. In other words, if I am merely material, my choices are solely a function of factors such as genetics and brain chemistry. The implications are profound. In a world that embraces fatalistic determinism, I cannot be held morally accountable for my actions, since reward and punishment make sense only if we have freedom of the will. Reason itself is reduced to the status of conditioned reflex. Moreover, the very concept of love is rendered meaningless. Rather than being the free act of a conscious will, love is relegated to a robotic procedure fatalistically determined by physical processes.[58]

In sum, purely naturalistic explanations, whether *psychopharmaco-logical*, *physiological*, or *psychological*, may account for the experience of autoscopic and transcendental episodes, but they do not account for consciousness in the first place. Despite the fact that near-death experiences are wildly divergent, subjective, and almost unanimously in conflict with a biblical understanding of death and the afterlife, they nonetheless serve to highlight the reality of consciousness.

WHAT DOES THE BIBLE SAY ABOUT NEAR-DEATH EXPERIENCES?

We must turn to the Bible because NDE advocates also turn to the Bible to support their interpretations of this phenomenon.

—J. ISAMU YAMAMOTO

If the Bible is clear about anything, it is that the human soul continues to exist after the death of the body. Moreover, according to Scripture, when Jesus appears a second time the souls of the departed will return to glorious resurrected bodies and we will evermore experience life *after* life-after-life. What the Bible does not address, however, is that which transpires during a near-death experience.

First, we should note that in his second letter to Corinthian Christians the apostle Paul makes clear that on five separate occasions Jewish leaders brought him to the very doorway of death through the horror of "the forty lashes minus one" (11:24). Not only so, says Paul, but "once I was stoned" (11:25). Dr. Luke chronicles this "near-death experience" in the fourteenth chapter of the Acts of the Apostles. At Lystra, a mob riled up by Jewish antagonists "stoned Paul and dragged him outside the city, thinking he was dead" (v. 19). While it may have been useful to concoct a miraculous resurrection from the dead in the narrative (after all, Paul had just healed a man who was lame from birth), Luke does no such thing. Instead, he matter-of-factly notes that Paul—revived from near-death—"got up and went back into the city. The next day he and Barnabas left for Derbe" (v. 20). One might well imagine Paul writing an epistle titled *From Lystra to Heaven*, but he did not so much as countenance the thought.

Furthermore, whether in Lystra or on a separate occasion, the apostle Paul speaks of being "caught up to the third heaven. Whether it was in the body or out of the body I do not know, but God knows," says Paul. In "paradise," he "heard inexpressible things, things that man is not permitted to tell." Paul humbly refrained from boasting about his celestial experience, so that "no one will think more of me than is warranted" (2 Corinthians 12:1–6). What we should note here is that Paul tacitly acknowledges that it is entirely possible to have an out-of-body experience. And if so, there is biblical precedence for contending that the soul continues to experience conscious awareness apart from the body. More importantly, however, we should note that in sharp contrast to modern near-death experiencers, Paul was not permitted to speak of his "surpassingly great revelations" (v. 7).

Finally, the incomparably great revelation of Scripture is this: "to live is Christ and to die is gain" (Philippians 1:21). Why? Because "away from the body" means "at home with the Lord" (2 Corinthians 5:8). Jesus is the prime exemplar. After his passion on the cross he cried out, "Father, into your hands I commit my spirit." And to the thief dying next to him he said, "I tell you the truth, today you will be with me in paradise" (Luke 23:43–46). In the transitional paradise that is what we will experience—like the thief and like Lazarus (Luke 16:25) we will be "comforted" (Luke 16:25). And in the eternal paradise, "the dwelling of God is with men, and he will live with them. They will be his people, and God himself will be with them and be their God. He will wipe every tear from their eyes. There will be no more death or mourning or crying or pain, for the old order of things has passed away" (Revelation 21:3–4). As eloquently summarized by the writer of Hebrews, "Christ was sacrificed once to take away the sins of many people; and he will appear a second time, not to bear sin, but to bring salvation to those who are waiting for him" (9:28).

In sum, near-death experiences add nothing whatsoever to the biblical portrayal of death and the afterlife. Instead, from Raymond Moody's *Life after Life* to Eban Alexander's *Proof of Heaven*, they sell sophistry, scriptorture, and even a dash of satanic subterfuge. "And no wonder, for Satan himself masquerades as an angel of light. It is not surprising, then, if his servants masquerade as servants of righteousness" (2 Corinthians 11:14–15). While it is not my place to judge motives—that is singularly the province of the Holy Spirit—I can say assuredly on the basis of Holy Scripture that the near-death experiences they chronicle tell us nothing whatsoever about what happens when we die. At best, they simply lend credence to the reality that the mind and the brain are not identical—and that is already buttressed by ample evidence.

CHAPTER
EIGHT

⋮

Is there a transitional hell?

IS THERE A DIFFERENCE BETWEEN HADES AND HELL?

The Greek word Hades (hadēs) is sometimes, but misleadingly, trans-lated "hell" in English versions of the New Testament.

—RICHARD BAUCKHAM

Christians have not always been cognizant of the biblical distinction between hades, the transitional hell depicted by our Lord in Luke 16; and the eternal hell, described by John in Revelation 20. In truth, as hor-rifying as hades is, it is an intermediate state—an earnest of hell. Hades differs from hell in several significant ways.

First, from the perspective of Scripture, hades is temporary, while hell is eternal. In Jesus' parable of the rich man and Lazarus, the rich man not only experiences torment in hades but begs Abraham to "send Lazarus to my father's house, for I have five brothers. Let him warn them, so that they will not also come to this place of torment" (Luke 16:27–28). Therefore, we are assured that the rich man is experiencing temporary torment in hades prior to the final judgment.

Furthermore, hades is torment in a disembodied state, while hell is torment in an embodied state after the second coming. In the words of Jesus, "Do not be amazed at this, for a time is coming when all who are in their graves will hear his voice and come out—those who have done good will rise to live, and those who have done evil will rise to be condemned" (John 5:28–29). The Master's words echo the prophetic words of Daniel, who wrote, "Multitudes who sleep in the dust of the earth will awake: some to everlasting life, others to shame and ever-lasting contempt" (Daniel 12:2). From such passages we may rightly conclude that those like the rich man who now experiences temporary torment in hades in a disembodied state will be resurrected to eternal torment in hell in a re-embodied state.

Finally, we see a distinction between hades and hell in that at the return of Christ the dead are judged according to what they have done. Then hades is thrown into hell (*gehenna*). Says John, "The sea gave up the dead that were in it, and death and Hades gave up the dead that were in them, and each person was judged according to what he had done. Then death and Hades were thrown into the lake of fire. The lake of fire is the second death" (Revelation 20:13–14).

In sum, hades is temporary torment in a disembodied state, while hell is the torment of being separated from the goodness and grace of God in the eternal state. Failure to make a distinction between hades and hell has led to myriad difficulties in biblical interpretation. As noted by Timothy Phillips in the *Evangelical Dictionary of Biblical Theology*, "Hades has only a limited existence; Gehenna or hell is the final place of judgment for the wicked. Many English versions foster confusion by translating both terms as 'hell.'"[1]

WHAT ABOUT PURGATORY?

As soon as the coin in the coffer rings,
the soul from purgatory springs.

—JOHANN TETZEL

Purgatory describes a place of purification. Roman Catholicism forwards the notion that there are specific sins that must be *purged* or *purified* "before the gates of heaven can be opened."[2] While Catholicism does not promote the gospel of the second chance, popular belief in purgatory is decidedly unbiblical.

First, the doctrine of purgatory, understood as post-death punishment or penance, undermines the sufficiency of Christ's atonement on the cross. Scripture declares that Christ through one sacrifice has made perfect forever those who are being made holy (Hebrews 10:14). Thus, we can rest assured that Christ received in his own body all the punishment we deserved, absolutely satisfying the justice of God on our behalf (Romans 3:25–26; 2 Corinthians 5:19, 21; 1 Peter 3:18; 1 John 2:2). When Jesus cried out from the cross, "It is finished!" (John 19:30) he was in effect saying, "The debt has been paid in full." Thus, no further debt need be paid in this life or in the life to come.

Furthermore, the Roman Catholic teaching that there are venial sins that can be expiated through temporal punishment in purgatory undermines the seriousness of sin. In reality, as the Bible makes clear, all our transgressions are sins against a holy, eternal God (Psalm 51:4). And as such, they rightly incur an eternal rather than a temporal debt—a debt paid once and for all by the perfect propitiating sacrifice of the spotless Lamb of God (John 1:29; Romans 6:23).

Finally, while purgatory was officially defined by the Council of Florence (1439) and officially defended by the Council of Trent in the late sixteenth century, nowhere is purgatory officially depicted in the canon of Scripture. As *The New Catholic Encyclopedia* readily acknowledges, "the doctrine of Purgatory is not explicitly stated in the Bible."[3] Thus, Catholicism is forced to appeal to the traditions of the Fathers rather than the testimony of the Father—who through his Word has graciously provided salvation by grace alone, through faith alone, on account of Christ alone (Romans 4:2–8; 11:6; Ephesians 2:8–9).

WHAT IS LIMBO?

Great grief seized on my heart when this I heard,
Because some people of much worthiness
I knew, who in that Limbo were suspended.

—DANTE

In popular culture *limbo* connotes a dance (for example, Chubby Checker singing, "How low can you go?"). In common parlance it denotes a suspended state—as in, "due to insufficient funds, comple-tion of the children's wing at Saint Regis is presently in a state of limbo." In Roman Catholic theology, however, *limbo* is quite literally the outer edge or boundary of hell. Catholics hold to the limbo of the patriarchs, the limbo of prebaptized infants, and the limbo of Pope John Paul II and Benedict XVI.

First, Roman Catholics have historically subscribed to what is known as the *limbo of the patriarchs* (*limbus partum*)—patriarchs like Abraham, Isaac, and Jacob, who died prior to Christ's passion on the cross. In this sense, Catholics hold to the notion of limbo as a temporary place for the souls of those who, having died in friendship with God, await "the harrowing of hell"[4]—during which the crucified Christ preached to spir-its in the realm of the dead. Thus, it may be said that Christ rescued the patriarchs and the penitent (e.g., the thief on the cross), gloriously ushering them from the boundary of hell into the hallowed regions of heaven.

Furthermore, there is the *limbo of the prebaptized infants*—those who die too young to be accountable for personal sins, yet who have not been absolved of original sin through the rite of baptism. As noted in the *Encyclopedia of Catholicism*, medieval theologians held that limbo "is a place or state where unbaptized persons enjoy a natural happiness, though they remain excluded from the Beatific Vision."[5] While deprived of the supernatural presence of God, such infants are believed to none-theless enjoy a state of maximal natural happiness and well-being on the hem of hell.

Finally, we should note the *limbo of Pope John Paul II and Benedict XVI*, who while affirming limbo as a credible theological possibility, nonetheless hopefully consider that infants—though they have not been baptized—may as yet be enjoying the Beatific Vision. Thus, in 2007, Pope Benedict XVI authorized publication of a document, originally commissioned by Pope John Paul II, titled *The Hope of Salvation for Infants Who Die without Being Baptized*. It should be emphasized that the present papal position is a prayerful hope rather than an absolute certainty.

Progression in Catholic theological reflection regarding limbo has enormous ramifications. Augustine contended that children who died prior to being baptized went straight to hell. "Medieval theologians, wishing to mitigate the harshness of Augustine's position, postulated the existence of limbo." And, "modern theology, when it does not reject the notion outright, questions the theological premises upon which limbo is based."[6] Therefore, Catholic parents may prayerfully hope that pre-baptized babies, previously believed to be excluded from heaven, may in reality be enjoying the presence of God. Moreover, in modern times babies who died prior to being baptized are not excluded from being buried in the consecrated grounds of Catholic cemeteries.

WHAT ABOUT GHOSTS?

During the fourth watch of the night Jesus went out to them, walking on the lake. When the disciples saw him walking on the lake, they were terrified. "It's a ghost," they said, and cried out in fear.

But Jesus immediately said to them: "Take courage! It is I. Don't be afraid."

—GOSPEL OF MATTHEW

The ghost of Kate Batts may well be the most-documented phantom in American history. So famous is the legend that, prior to becoming president, Andrew Jackson is said to have investigated this notorious poltergeist (noisy ghost) himself. While the legend continues to be sustained by sophists, sensationalists, and storytellers, Scripture hardly supports the notion that spirits of the dead can return to harass the living.

First, as the Bible makes clear, souls of the departed are either comforted in the presence of God or in agony absent his loving presence.

Such is the case, as we have seen, in Luke 16. Upon death, the soul of Lazarus experienced comfort in Abraham's bosom. Conversely, the soul of the rich man experienced torment in hades. Neither was permitted to return to the land of the living.

Moreover, the very notion of communicating with the dead (necromancy) is denounced in Scripture. Thus, when the departed Samuel appeared to the living Saul, the witch of Endor immediately recognized the occasion as a non-normative act of God—a divine display of judgment rather than a haunting (1 Samuel 28:3–25). While the witch may have been able to delude the gullible via the guise of conjuring, she was far from self-deluded. She was well aware of the fact that Samuel's appearance in the land of the living was in spite of her deceptions, not because of them. While she trafficked in delusion and the demonic, she was wholly incapable of conjuring up the ghosts of the departed.

Furthermore, as delineated in Scripture, ghosts are the stuff of superstition. Yet, as in ancient Israel, such superstition is the stock-in-trade of modern culture. The gullible have turned from God to ghosts in incessant inquiries concerning the gloom that lies ahead. In reality, necromancy is a devilish deception. What foolishness to feign communication with the dead in the guise of enlightening those who dwell in the land of the living! Says the prophet Isaiah, "When men tell you to consult mediums and spiritists, who whisper and mutter, should not a people inquire of their God?" (8:19).

Those not bound to Scripture are bound to sink in superstition. Even the disciples, when they saw Jesus walking toward them on the sea, momentarily submerged themselves in superstition (Matthew 14:26). Had they clung to the Scripture in the midst of swirling doubts, they would not so much as given voice to their latent superstitions. Just as Lazarus was not permitted to return to the land of the living, so the Scriptures make clear that the dead do not inhabit this realm. The very notion is "detestable to the Lord" (Deuteronomy 18:12).

Finally, we should note that while the spirits of the dead do not inhabit the land of the living, demonic spirits are pleased to play on the field of superstition. Ghosts exist only in mythology, but demons are more than happy to feed our unbiblical delusions. While fallen angels are not physical, they are as real as the very flesh upon our bones. No doubt much to his delight, the devil is forever portrayed as a cartoonish clown with an elongated tail, red tights, and a pitchfork. Far from silly or stupid, however, Satan appears as a cosmopolitan angel of enlightenment. He knows full well that without the spiritual armor listed by Paul in Ephesians 6, we are but pawns in a devil's game.

With this in mind, Paul warns us to "be alert and always keep on praying for all the saints" (v. 18). His words hearken back to the admonition of the Master, who warned the slumbering disciples, "Watch and pray so that you will not fall into temptation" (Matthew 26:41). Peter extends the warning by urging us to "be self-controlled and alert. Your enemy the devil prowls around like a roaring lion looking for someone to devour. Resist him, standing firm in the faith" (1 Peter 5:8–9).

If we lose the ability to think biblically, we will quickly be transformed from cultural change agents and initiators into cultural conformists and imitators—from God-bearers to "ghostbusters."

CAN RESURRECTION AND REINCARNATION BE HARMONIZED?

Many Christians have misconceptions about reincarnation. One particular misconception is that it means people don't inhabit heavenly realms between Earth lives. The misconception is that people reincarnate immediately after death. It ignorantly assumes people will never be permanent residents of heavenly realms. But near-death testimony reveals these misconceptions to be just that—misconceptions. People are free to spend an "eternity of eternities" in afterlife realms before reincarnating to Earth again.

—KEVIN WILLIAMS

The Eastern world has long considered reincarnation—literally, rebirth in another body—to be a universal law of life. Millions of Buddhists, Hindus, Sikhs, and Jains hold reincarnation to be inexorable truth—as inviolate as the law of gravity. Consequently, it is not at all surprising to find a cow in Calcutta afforded more consideration than a child. What is surprising is the vast rapidity with which belief in reincarnation has grown in the West where asking about your past lives is about as common as asking whether you are a Leo or a Libra. Incredibly, being born again in another body is now the theology du jour of approximately one out of every ten church attendees.[7] Indeed, many go so far as to contend that reincarnation is a thoroughly biblical proposition. Which begs the question, can reincarnation be harmonized with resurrection?

First, as should be obvious, the biblical view of *one death* per person can never rightly be reconciled with reincarnation's dogma of an ongoing cycle of death and rebirth. As Scripture makes plain, we are "destined to die *once*, and after that to face judgment" (Hebrews 9:27). In contrast to being born again and again and again in various bodies, the Christian worldview maintains that the souls of believers will be reunited with resurrected bodies transformed from mortality to immortality.

Being *born again* and *being born again in another body* may sound alike but are as different as day is from night. To be *born again* is to be reborn spiritually. As Jesus said to Nicodemus, "Flesh gives birth to flesh, but the Spirit gives birth to spirit" (John 3:6). To be *born again in another body* involves the endless transmigration of the soul. According to *Time* magazine, Shirley MacLaine and Sylvester Stallone both believe they were beheaded, "she by Louis XV, he during the French Revolution. Stallone thinks he may have been a monkey in Guatemala, and MacLaine is sure she was a prostitute in a previous life."[8] Both are no doubt hopeful their souls will not return in the bodies of mice or misfits.

Furthermore, the biblical maxim of *one body* per person demonstrates that the chasm between reincarnation and resurrection can never be bridged. Rather than the *transmigration* of our souls into different bodies, the apostle Paul professes that Christ "will *transform* our lowly bodies" (Philippians 3:21). As Paul explicitly explains, the body that dies is the body that rises. "The body that is sown is perishable, *it* is raised imperishable; it is sown in dishonor, *it* is raised in glory; it is sown in weakness, *it* is raised in power; it is sown a natural body, *it* is raised a spiritual body" (1 Corinthians 15:42–44).

No longer will our bodies be *simply natural*. Instead, they will be *supernatural*. As we've seen, our resurrection bodies will be gloriously dominated by the Holy Spirit rather than by hedonistic sensations. In place of "sexual immorality, impurity and debauchery; idolatry and witchcraft; hatred, discord, jealousy, fits of rage, selfish ambition, dissensions, factions and envy; drunkenness, orgies, and the like" (Galatians 5:19–21), we will faithfully manifest the fruit of the Spirit, which is "love, joy, peace, patience, kindness, goodness, faithfulness, gentleness and self-control" (vv. 22–23). Put another way, our spiritual bodies will be supernatural, Spirit dominated, and sin-free.

Finally, the Christian belief that there is only one way to God categorically demonstrates that resurrection and reincarnation can never be reconciled. Says Christ, "I am *the* way and *the* truth and *the* life. No one comes to the Father except through me" (John 14:6). Since Christ can be demonstrated to be truly God, his claim to be the only way must be taken seriously. Only if he were merely one in a pantheon of pretenders could his proclamations be pushed aside. That is precisely why the resurrection is axiomatic to Christianity. Through his resurrection Christ demonstrated that he does not stand in a line of peers with Buddha, Baha'u'llah, Krishna, or any other founder of a world religion. They died and are *still* dead, but Christ is risen—he is risen indeed.

While reincarnation in the West is as prevalent on Main Street as it is in mainstream movies, it hardly comports with reality. To murder a mosquito, even in self-defense, is hardly equivalent to taking the life of a previous person. And Sylvester Stallone was hardly monkeyed around—at least not in a previous life. The reality is, resurrection and reincarnation can never be reconciled because the former is a historical fact while the latter is nothing more than a Hindu fantasy.

DID JEREMIAH, JOHN, AND JESUS HOLD TO REINCARNATION?

Souls are poured from one into another of different kinds of bodies of the world.
—WORDS PUT INTO THE MOUTH OF JESUS CHRIST IN THE GNOSTIC
(AND FALSE) GOSPEL PISTIS SOPHIA

The year 1893 brought a paradigm shift to the West. Buddhists, Baha'is and Bhahti Yogis from the East arrived in Chicago to attend the inaugural Parliament of World Religions. Though their contingent was sizable, they were vastly outnumbered by Western Bible believers. Despite the disparity in numbers, however, the impact of the Eastern contingent was monumental. Swami Vivekananda, a disciple of the self-proclaimed "godman" Sri Ramakrishna, skillfully used the parliament to sow the seeds for a new global spirituality—a spirituality supplanting the doctrine of resurrection with the dogma of reincarnation. One hundred years later—at the centennial celebration of the original Parliament of World Religions—the impact of Vivekananda's message was seen in living color. Buddhists outnumbered Baptists, and saffron robes were more common than Christian clerical clothing. Even more telling, multitudes in the church and in the culture had concluded that the Bible might actually be reconciled to the concept of reincarnation. Incredibly, the words of Jeremiah, John, and Jesus came to be touted in evidence.

First, in Jeremiah, God allegedly tells his prophet that he knew him as the result of a prior incarnation: "Before I formed you in the womb I knew you, before you were born I set you apart; I appointed you as a prophet to the nations" (Jeremiah 1:5). Far from suggesting that his prophet had existed in a prior incarnation, however, this passage makes clear that the One who has existed throughout eternity set Jeremiah apart for a special prophetic task.

Those familiar with their Bible know immediately that God's knowledge concerning Jeremiah was far from unique. Like Samson, who was foreknown "to be a Nazirite, set apart to God from birth" (Judges 13:5), Jeremiah was set apart for a special commission in the economy of God. Thus, as Samson was equipped to carry out his calling, God assures Jeremiah that he would not fail to equip him with prophetic prowess. Like them, you and I are not only chosen by God but commissioned by God to carry out the unique calling of God in the ushering in of the kingdom of God—in this, not a future incarnation.

Furthermore, reincarnationists are predisposed to citing a passage in the gospel of John in which the disciples are said to wonder whether a man born blind is paying off karmic debt for himself or for his parents (John 9:1–2). In other words, the man is allegedly blind for something he did in a prior incarnation. Thus, they believe his blindness is a function of karma—the law of moral causation.

Far from giving credence to such morbid considerations, the gospel of John clearly dispels all such mythological speculation by overtly stating that the blindness of the man in question had nothing to do with either his personal sin or that of his parents (John 9:3). Moreover, had the blind man really been suffering on account of past indiscretions, Jesus would have violated the law of karma by healing him.

Finally, in Matthew's gospel, Jesus is cited as suggesting that Elijah was reincarnated as John the Baptist (Matthew 11:14). Context, however, tells a far different story. When the priests and Levites asked John if he was Elijah, he replied, "I am not" (John 1:21). Elijah and John are not said to be two incarnations of the same person, but two separate people functioning in a strikingly similar prophetic role. As Dr. Luke put it: John the Baptist came "in the spirit and power of Elijah" (1:17).

One thing is certain: reincarnation is wholly inconsistent with a biblical view of reality. As we have seen, in his parable concerning the rich man and Lazarus, Jesus describes the horrors of judgment in the after-life, rather than the horrors of karmic debt in another life (Luke 16). The writer of Hebrews unambiguously declares that human beings are "destined to die once, and after that to face judgment" (9:27).

DID JESUS GO TO HELL?

There is no textual basis in the New Testament for claiming that between Good Friday and Easter Christ was preaching to souls impris-oned in hell or Hades. There is textual basis for saying that he would be with the repentant thief in Paradise "today" (Luke 23:43), and one does not get the impression that he means a defective place from which the thief must then be delivered by more preaching.

—JOHN PIPER

For many the question of whether Jesus went to hell may seem odd. Yet it is a question in desperate need of an answer. Not only because millions invoke the phrase "he descended into hell" as they recite the Apostles' Creed, but because many more have been taught that after death Jesus descended into hell in order to proclaim his victory over fallen angels who had violated women prior to Noah's flood or, as some say, to preach to human spirits held captive by death and the grave. Multiplied millions have been caught up in the notion that their redemption was secured in an epic battle between Satan and the Savior in the cauldron of hell. One popular Word of Faith teacher goes so far as to ask, "Do you think that the punishment for our sin was to die on a cross? If that were the case, the two thieves could have paid your price. No, the punishment was to go to hell itself and to serve time in hell separated from God."[9] While none of the aforementioned explanations—save the last—approaches the level of heresy, all are based on texts taken out of context. Three in particular are of note.

First, we read in 1 Peter 3:19–20 that Jesus "went and preached to the spirits in prison who disobeyed long ago when God waited patiently in the days of Noah while the ark was being built." While various paradigms have been imposed on this passage, two have become extraordinarily popular.

One is that Jesus descended into hell to preach to "spirits in prison" who had impregnated fallen females during the days prior to Noah's flood (Genesis 6:1–4). This is untenable for a variety of reasons. Demons are nonsexual, nonphysical beings and as such are incapable of having sexual relations and producing physical offspring. To say that demons can create bodies with DNA and fertile sperm is to say that demons have creative power—which is an exclusively divine prerogative. While angels can materialize by God's creative power, demons have no such prerogative. Moreover, if demons could have sex with women in ancient times, we would have no assurance they could not do so in modern times. Nor would we have any guarantee that the people we encounter every day are fully human. As Genesis 1 makes plain, all of God's living creations are designed to reproduce "according to their own *kinds*" (vv. 11–12, 21, 24–25 ESV).

The other popular paradigm imposed on the Peter passage in question is the notion that during the three days between his death and resurrection, Jesus went to hell to finish the work of redemption. Word of Faith teacher Kenneth Copeland is emphatic: "When Jesus cried, 'It is finished!' he was not speaking of the plan of redemption. There were still three days and nights to go through before he went to the throne." Copeland continues, "Jesus' death on the cross was only the beginning of the complete work of redemption."[10]

This, however, is far from true. The glorious message of atonement is that the unblemished Lamb fully paid for sin through his passion on the cross. As such, each time we take Communion, we remember his broken body and his shed blood for the *complete* remission of sin. When Jesus, on the cross, uttered the words, "It is finished!" (John 19:30), no further debt remained. Indeed, the Greek word—*tetelestai*—literally means, "It is paid; the debt has been paid in full" (cf. Hebrews 9:1–14, 10:19–22). To say otherwise is an atonement atrocity amounting to full-blown heresy.[11]

So if Peter does not intend to communicate that Jesus descended into hell to complete the work of atonement, what does he intend to communicate? The answer is this: just as the Spirit of Jesus preached through Noah to the people of his day—who were then in the flesh, but at the writing of Peter's epistles were disembodied spirits incarcerated in the prison house of hades—so too in the days preceding the fall of Jerusalem, the Spirit of Jesus was preaching through Peter and the persecuted to a pagan world drowning in a flood of dissipation.

The parallels between the day of Noah and Peter's day are striking. Like Noah and his family, the faithful were an insignificant minority in the midst of a wicked and perverse generation (Genesis 6:5–8). Moreover, as Noah built the ark believing that he would see God's judgment befall the wicked within his own lifetime, so Peter proclaimed that scoffers would witness the destruction of Jerusalem within their very own generation. As the world was deluged and destroyed in the days of Noah, so Jerusalem and its glorious temple were "reserved for fire" in the day of a fledgling first-century church (2 Peter 3:7). As Noah "condemned the world and became heir of the righteousness that comes by faith" (Hebrews 11:7), and as the persecuted in Peter's day were "being built into a spiritual house to be a holy priesthood" (1 Peter 2:5), so too we are exhorted to look forward in faith to an ultimate "day of the Lord" in which "the elements will be destroyed by fire, and the earth and everything in it will be laid bare. . . . But in keeping with his promise . . . a new heaven and a new earth, the home of righteousness," will gloriously emerge out of the ashes of devastation (2 Peter 3:10, 13).

In sum, 1 Peter 3:19 has nothing whatsoever to do with Jesus going to hell during the days between his death and resurrection to preach to demonic spirits or to disobedient scoffers who disobeyed while the ark was being built. Instead, the disobedient who died in Noah's day, in Peter's day and who die in our day comprise "the spirits in prison" (souls in hades) who await a final Day of Judgment in which they will be summarily sentenced and sent to an eternal prison designated in Scripture as hell.

Furthermore, as with the words of Peter, so too the words of Paul written in his epistle to Ephesian Christians are frequently taken to communicate that Jesus descended into hell: "What does 'he ascended' mean except that he also descended to the lower, earthly regions? He who descended is the very one who ascended higher than all the heavens, in order to fill the whole universe" (4:9–10). The question is, do the phrases, "he also descended to the lower earthly regions" and "he descended into hell" have equivalent meanings?

The unequivocal answer is—*no!* Far from demonstrating that our Lord went to hell, this passage contains an idiomatic expression (an expression unique to the Greek), referring to Christ's incarnation on earth. In evidence, David uses the selfsame expression ("lower parts" or "depths of the earth") in exclaiming, "My frame was not hidden from you when I was made in the secret place. When I was woven together *in the depths of the earth*, your eyes saw my unformed body" (Psalm 139:15–16). Surely no one rightly supposes that David was born in the dungeons of hell! Indeed, far from crying out something like, "Satan into thy hellish clutches I submit my being," as Word of Faith teachers would like to have it, Christ cried from the cross, "Father into your hands I commit my spirit" (Luke 23:46; cf. John 19:30). As such, he did not spend three days between death and resurrection experiencing the horror of hell; rather, absent from the body, he was immediately present with the Father in heaven.

Finally, the words of Jesus—"As Jonah was three days and three nights in the belly of a huge fish, so the Son of Man will be three days and three nights in the heart of the earth" (Matthew 12:40)—have been twisted in an attempt to shore up the notion that between death and resurrection, Jesus "descended into hell."

While the phrase "heart of the earth" has been taken to mean the cauldron of hell, in reality Christ was speaking of his death and burial in the tomb of Joseph of Arimathea. Jonah's entombment in the stomach of a fish was the type; Jesus' entombment in the sepulchre of a friend, the antitype. Moreover, there is not even a hint in Matthew's gospel, or for that matter in the rest of Scripture, that Jesus experienced three days and three nights in mortal combat with the forces of darkness. Nor is there any warrant for supposing that *hades* is located in the heart or the core of the earth.

I would be remiss at this point if I failed to mention that Word of Faith proponents often wrongly argue that the belief that Christ suffered under the demonic hosts in hell is consistent with early apostolic teaching. In doing so, they invoke the phrase "he descended into hell" from the oldest rule of faith—the Apostles' Creed.

This, however, is hardly a convincing argument. Prior to its crystallization as a confession, the creed was used in rudimentary permutations as a *rite of baptism*—but without the phrase in question. The creed began to take on permanency as a *rule of faith* because of Gnostic heresies that arose in the early Christian church prior to the middle of the second century—but still without the phrase "he descended into hell."

Even in form of the Old Roman Creed, codified by Bishop Marcellus of Ancyra in the late fourth century, the confession did not contain the phrase "he descended into hell." Indeed, not until standardization as the Received Creed long after the fourth century was the clause appended to the confession—and perhaps not officially so until the eighth century. Moreover, we should note that even had the clause been invoked by the early Christian church, the intent would not have been to communicate that Jesus finished the work of redemption in hell.

If church history tells us anything, it is that the early Christians celebrated the broken body and shed blood of Christ on the cross for the *complete* remission of their sins.

WHY DOES THE APOSTLES' CREED SAY THAT JESUS "DESCENDED INTO HELL"?

I believe in God, the Father Almighty,
the Maker of heaven and earth,
and in Jesus Christ, His only Son, our Lord:
Who was conceived by the Holy Ghost,
born of the virgin Mary,
suffered under Pontius Pilate,
was crucified, dead, and buried;
He descended into hell.
The third day He arose again from the dead;
He ascended into heaven,
and sitteth on the right hand of God the Father Almighty;
from thence He shall come to judge the quick and the dead.
I believe in the Holy Ghost;
the holy catholic church;
the communion of saints;
the forgiveness of sins;
the resurrection of the body;
and the life everlasting.
Amen.

—APOSTLES' CREED

The Apostles' Creed is no doubt the most precise and poetic summary of the Christian faith in existence. As the Nicene Creed is emblematic of the Eastern Church, so the Apostles' Creed is emblematic of the Western Church. Nonetheless, the phrase "he descended into hell"—which is not in the Nicene Creed—is highly controversial. Some Christians remove it, others reinterpret it, and still others simply refuse to recite it. Given the controversy, one wonders how the phrase came to be included in the creed to begin with.

First, it is instructive to understand how the Apostles' Creed morphed into existence. As I have previously pointed out, prior to crystallization as a creedal confession in public worship, it was recited as a rite of baptism.[12] In the middle of the second century, such recitations were systematized as a rule of faith due to Gnostic heresies that threatened to subvert essential Christian doctrine. In the fourth century, it was codified in the Greek by Marcellus of Ancyra and in the Latin by Rufinus of Aquileia. Not until standardization as the Received Creed, long after the fourth century, was the clause "he descended into hell" appended to the confession—and perhaps not officially so until the eighth century.[13] One thing is certain: because the phrase in question did not appear in the Apostles' Creed until late, it cannot be credibly argued that it was the profession of early church fathers—much less the apostles.

Furthermore, the phrase in question resulted from misinterpretations of biblical passages such as 1 Peter 3:19. Augustine, who on the basis of the Peter passage, believed that in some sense Jesus preached to spirits in prison, candidly wondered why he would have preached only to the disobedient of Noah's day.[14] Changing conceptions concerning the nature of hell only complicated matters. Traditions concerning limbo and purgatory caused Aquinas to wonder which realm of the dead Jesus preached to and who, if anyone, was saved. In the end he supposed that Christ may well have proclaimed final condemnation in the realm of the wicked and in the regions of purgatory the hope of glory.[15] For his part, Calvin solved the conundrum by interpreting the descent into hell as symbolic of Christ's passion.[16] Such scholastic analysis and rational interpretation proved unsatisfying in the Eastern Church. Thus, the preaching of Christ "to the spirits in prison" remained a mystery that

Eastern believers indulged in the spirit of liturgy but never pontificated as a rational creed. One thing is certain: neither the Eastern Church nor the Western Church adopted the Word of Faith predilection that Jesus went to hell to serve our sentence at the hands of so-called satanic torturers.

Finally, the phrase "he descended into hell" may well have been included in the creed due to a misapprehension of meaning respecting *hades* and *hell*. As noted by Philip Schaff in *The Creeds of Christendom*, the word *hell* with all its connotations was likely inadvertently substituted for the word *hades* in the creeds.[17] As is the case today, Christians have not always been cognizant of the biblical distinction between hades, as depicted by our Lord in Luke 16, and hell as described by John in passages such as Revelation 20. Put another way, from the perspective of Scripture, hades and gehenna (i.e., hell) are not synonymous. Indeed, as horrifying as hades is, it is but an earnest of gehenna, to which the rich man will be sentenced when Jesus appears a second time. As such, the apostle John describes the horror of hades being thrown into the lake of fire (hell) in terms of "the second death" (Revelation 20:14).

In any case, the canon of Scripture, not the Apostles' Creed, is the final court of arbitration. How can anyone miss what our Lord said to the thief on the cross: "I tell you the truth, today you will be with me in paradise" (Luke 23:43)? As such, the phrase "he descended into hell" is a mistaken tradition, a misunderstanding of Scripture, and a misapprehension of the meaning of words.

PART THREE

⋮

Life: What You Do Now Counts for All Eternity

All of us presently live in that dash between the date of our birth and the date of our death. For some the dash is short, for others, a bit longer. But for all of us, that tiny dash represents the duration of our present life on earth. My dad was born five years after the First World War (1923) and died in 1997. Thus, the dash on his tombstone already has four digits on either side of it. I was born five years after the Second World War (1950). And my dash is as yet followed by a question mark. What is true for me is likewise true for everyone reading these words. Whether you are old or young, rich or poor, male or female, you light the sky for the briefest of moments. And then eternity.

In the meantime, what you and I do today, this week, this month, this year, will have direct consequences for all eternity. Thus, while culture seeks to focus your gaze on greatness—Christianity rightly focuses your gaze on grace and godliness. Think for a moment about the "greats" in the celebrated history of humanity. From the perspective of life and legacy Cyrus the Great was a veritable superstar—the embodiment of a kingdom of bronze that would "rule over the whole earth" (Daniel 2:39). As Belshazzar drank wine from Jerusalem's gold and silver goblets, Cyrus diverted the Euphrates and stole into Babylon. Belshazzar was slain and citizens of a golden empire now in disarray embraced him as liberator. In biblical parlance, it was the edict of Cyrus that fulfilled the prophetic words of Jeremiah: "When seventy years are completed for Babylon, I will come to you and fulfill my gracious promise to bring you back to this place" (Jeremiah 29:10). Yet in spite of the most celebrated edict in the history of humanity and an empire that was not eclipsed until the time of the Romans, Cyrus was dead scarcely nine years after overwhelming Babylon, glory of the Chaldeans.

Alexander the Great, like Cyrus, is immortalized in the annals of history. Astride his mighty black steed Bucephalus, its massive brow adorned by a glistening white star, he sent tremors of terror down the spines of the Medo-Persian military. When Darius III offered Alexander the entirety of the Persian Empire west of the Euphrates in return for peace, he merely responded in bloody pursuit. Alexander defeated Darius at Gaugamela and there, in concert with the prophecies of Daniel, became supreme monarch of the ancient world. After destroying Tyre, the great Phoenician capital of the ancient world, Alexander crucified two thousand Tyrians and established Alexandria as the commercial capital of the ancient world. Yet in keeping with Daniel's prophetic words, "at the height of his power his large horn was broken off, and in its place four prominent horns grew up toward the four winds of heaven" (Daniel 8:8). One month shy of his thirty-third birthday Alexander the Great, who allegedly wept because there were no more kingdoms to conquer, was dead.

As "the large horn" prophesied by Daniel was Alexander the Great, the "horn, which started small" but "grew until it reached the host of the heavens" was Antiochus IV Epiphanes, king of the north and chief villain of the Greco-Syrian Empire (Daniel 8:9–10). Daniel describes Antiochus as a beast that would trample its foes underfoot; as a little horn that would grow in power and become the greatest of four kings; and as a master of intrigue who would ruthlessly oppress the saints for a time, times, and a division of time. He mercilessly crucified Jews in Jerusalem for resisting his inexorable Hellenization advances and in superhuman arrogance declared himself the incarnation of Zeus, father of the gods. Yet barely three and a half years after he had accomplished his mission to desecrate the temple fortress, abolish the daily sacrifice, and set up the abomination that causes desolation, the Syrian beast, like Cyrus and Alexander before him, was dead.[1]

John the Baptist, too, was great—but in a far different sense. He did not wear fine clothes or live in a palace. Nor was he ruler of an expansive empire. Yet the Creator of heaven and earth afforded him the ultimate commendation. "Among those born of women there has not risen one *greater* than John the Baptist" (Matthew 11:11 NKJV). Indeed, who could be greater than John, the last of the Old Testament prophets? The Elijah who was to come. The very one the prophet Malachi had famously predicted would prepare the way for the King of kings and the Lord of lords (Malachi 3:1). Cyrus, Alexander, and Antiochus ruled this world. John the Baptist prepared the way for the world that is to come. Though he was beheaded in the prime of his life, John the Baptist had extreme significance for both time and for eternity.

Despite John's greatness, Jesus said the "least in the kingdom of heaven is greater than he" (Matthew 11:11). How can that be? How can one like you or me be greater than the one of whom Christ said "among those born of women there has not risen one greater than John the Baptist" (NKJV)? The answer is this: the Old Testament prophets predicted the coming of Christ; the last of them prepared the way for him. But you and I live between the inauguration of the kingdom of heaven and the consummation when heaven and earth are joined as one. Jesus lived, died, rose from the dead, and transcended time and space.

But you and I live in this space-time continuum. We have been left as Messiah's mediators. Mediators by which this present universe is to be transformed. "Enemy occupied territory," said C. S. Lewis, "that is what this world is. Christianity is the story of how the rightful king has landed in disguise, and is calling us to take part in a great campaign of sabotage."[2]

It is not as though we are waiting to be raptured out of this world. No! You and I are not going anywhere! Heaven and earth have been conjoined. Jesus is coming back. As the inspired writer of Hebrews puts it, "he will appear a second time, not to bear sin, but to bring salvation to those who are waiting for him" (9:28). And when he appears again heaven and earth will be as one—united, as it was before the advent of decay, disease, destruction, and death. The dwelling of God will be here, not there. As John so wonderfully promises, God himself will live with saved humanity. "They will be his people, and God himself will be with them and be their God" (Revelation 21:3).

What this means for you and me is that our present life matters. We are not going to be resurrected to another world. We await our resurrection in this world! This world is not about to be scrapped; it will ultimately be redeemed. And we are partakers in the process. That is precisely what the Apostle to the Gentiles means in saying that "the creation waits in eager expectation for the sons of God to be revealed" Romans 8:19). Do you get that? Creation and its crowning jewels will be revealed in splendor. I love what N. T. Wright writes in *Surprised by Hope*: God does not want "to rescue humans *from* creation any more than he wanted to rescue Israel *from* the Gentiles. He wanted to rescue Israel *in order that Israel might be a light to the Gentiles*, and he wanted thereby to rescue humans *in order that humans might be his rescuing stewards over creation*."[3]

Your greatness is not a function of stuff or status. It is forever a feature of being a son or daughter in the kingdom of heaven—now inaugurated, one day consummated. We do not pray, "Thy kingdom come,

Thy will be done in earth, as it is in heaven" in vain (Matthew 6:10 KJV). Nor do we pray passively. We are mediators of God's redemption— rescuing stewards of creation. As such, the words of Jesus have personal application: "You have been faithful with a few things; I will put you in charge of many things. Come and share your master's happiness!" (Matthew 25:21).

We have been called to fulfill the Great Commission and have been commissioned to fulfill the cultural mandate. We have been called to be "Christ's ambassadors, as though God were making his appeal through us" (2 Corinthians 5:20), but we are also commanded to "be fruitful and increase in number; fill the earth and subdue it. Rule over the fish of the sea and the birds of the air and over every living creature that moves on the ground" (Genesis 1:28). In essence, you and I are being honed as caretakers of a restored garden.

Make no mistake. Paradise lost will one day be paradise restored. In the words of cultural apologist Nancy Pearcey, we are to "develop the social world: build families, churches, schools, cities, governments, laws" as well as "plant crops, build bridges, design computers, compose music."[4] In other words, as "Sons of God" we are to care for the created order. In an age in which Christians are all-too-often characterized as "poor, undereducated, and easily led,"[5] we should avoid lending credence to the stereotype. Instead, we should commit ourselves to care for Christ's creation with tender hearts as well as with tenacious minds.

Realize the significance of your life in the here and now. It really does matter! An important question posed in part 3 is this: "What must I do to inherit eternal life?" In the dash between date of birth and date of death, this question is paramount in the whole of that which faces humanity. Once the ultimate question of life is settled, the question of life after life as well as life *after* life-after-life is pregnant with promise.

CHAPTER
NINE

⋮

Doesn't a loving God want everyone in heaven?

WILL EVERYONE ULTIMATELY GO TO HEAVEN?

A staggering number of people have been taught that a select few Christians will spend forever in a peaceful, joyous place called heaven, while the rest of humanity spends forever in torment and punishment in hell with no chance for anything better. It's been clearly communicated to many that this belief is the central truth of the Christian faith and to reject it is, in essence, to reject Jesus. This is misguided and toxic.

—ROB BELL

At first blush this may seem a strange question, but in reality it may well be *the* question of the day. Will everyone go to heaven? Christian author Rob Bell answers this question in two words: *Love Wins.* In his bestseller by the same title, Bell suggests that everyone from Ghandi to God-denying atheists will likely end up in heaven. Why? Because love wins! To believe otherwise is to hold to a monstrous God—a being who could never be trusted, let alone be good—*"a cruel, mean, vicious tormenter."*[1] A God who is loving one moment, vicious the next. Bell's outrage against such a God is palpable. "If there was an earthly father who was like that, we would call the authorities. If there was an actual human dad who was that volatile, we would contact child protection services immediately."[2]

Bell is equally outraged by those who believe in the concept of eternal separation. "If your God will punish people for all of eternity for sins committed in a few short years," there is something so drastically wrong that no amount of "clever marketing or compelling language" can camouflage it.[3] To correct this "wrong," Bell markets a God perfectly suited for what J. I. Packer dubbed "a post-Christian, human-centered, self-absorbed, feel-good, secular culture."[4]

Bell begins his diatribe against the reality of hell with the story of a church attendee who had the temerity to connect Mahatma Gandhi with the word *hell.* Bell's response? "Really? Gandhi's in hell? He is? We have confirmation of this? Somebody knows this? Without a doubt? And that somebody decided to take on the responsibility of letting the rest of us know? Of all the billions of people who have ever lived, will only a select number 'make it to a better place' and every single other person suffer in torment and punishment forever?"[5]

What the church attendee found unquestionable raised a veritable storm of questions for Bell. "Has God created millions of people over tens of thousands of years who are going to spend eternity in anguish? Can God do this, or even allow this, and still claim to be a loving God? Does God punish people for thousands of years with infinite, eternal torment for things they did in their few finite years of life?"[6]

If so, Bell has a painfully simple solution: terminate children before they reach the age of accountability. "If every new baby being born could grow up to *not* believe the right things and go to hell forever, then prematurely terminating a child's life anytime from conception to twelve years of age would actually be the loving thing to do, guaranteeing that the child ends up in heaven, and not hell, forever. Why run the risk?"[7] While Bell sits in judgment over his church attendee, perhaps he should reconsider his own judgment.

First, imagine the leap of logic Bell is taking. Imagine suggesting that were hell a possibility for Gandhi, then terminating a child's life might be the most loving thing to do. While the attendee may have been ill-advised to say Gandhi was destined for hell, Bell is ill-advised to rebuke a God who would allow Gandhi to choose hell and "still claim to be a loving God."

Bell's church attendee is in no position to judge Gandhi—but then, neither is Bell. What *can* be tested are Gandhi's beliefs. Gandhi considered the deity of Jesus Christ and summarily dismissed it. "I cannot ascribe exclusive divinity to Jesus. He is as divine as Krishna or Rama or Mohammed or Zoroaster."[8] He read the Bible and deemed it "as much a book of religion with me as the Gita and the Koran."[9] He measured the miracles of Jesus and said, "He brought to life not people who were dead but who were believed to be dead. The laws of Nature are changeless, unchangeable and there are no miracles in the sense of infringement or interruption of Nature's laws."[10]

While Bell registers shock over his attendee's assumptions respecting Gandhi's eternal destiny, in reality they are hardly surprising. Given a worldview that embraces the deity of Christ, elevates the Bible as divine rather than merely human in origin, expects the miraculous, and exalts an objective standard of morality, the attendee's perspective is not particularly shocking. What is shocking is Bell's dogmatic dismissal of hell itself—especially in light of that which is clear in Scripture. Christ, in his Olivet Discourse, equated the eternality of hell to that of heaven in saying that the unrighteous "will go away to *eternal* punishment, but the righteous to *eternal* life" (Matthew 25:46).

Furthermore, it may not be too much to say that Gandhi is the smokescreen; Bell's real objection is hell's *eternality*. To say Bell goes to elaborate lengths to undermine *forever* is hardly an overstatement. Respecting the aforementioned words of Christ in the Olivet Discourse, he writes, "When we read 'eternal punishment,' it's important that we don't read categories and concepts into a phrase that aren't there. Jesus isn't talking about forever as we think of forever." Indeed, says Bell, "'forever' is not really a category the biblical writers used."[11] Moreover, "the goats" referred to by Jesus "are sent, in the Greek language, to an *aion* of *kolazo*. *Aion*, we know, has several meanings. One is 'age' or 'period of time'; another refers to intensity of experience. The word *kolazo* is a term from horticulture. It refers to the pruning and the trimming of the branches of a plant so it can flourish." So, the hell of Bell is "a time of trimming."[12]

While the average church attendee may feel inept to counter Bell's erudite articulation of the original languages, in reality common sense is all that is necessary. If Bell is right in suggesting that *eternal punishment* is a temporary time of pruning (think purgatory), then by the same token eternal life is temporary as well. The Bible as a whole is unambiguous respecting the nature of eternity. Biblical exegesis yields neither universalism, annihilationism, nor postmortem evangelism. Rather, as Paul makes clear, "those who do not know God and do not obey the gospel of our Lord Jesus" will be eternally separated from his goodness and grace. "They will be punished with *everlasting* destruction and *shut out from the presence of the Lord* and from the majesty of his power" (2 Thessalonians 1:9). The language of "destruction" here does not connote annihilation but rather evokes the horror of what it will be for the unrighteous to experience eternal eradication of the image of God—now stained but then erased, as "brute beasts, creatures of instinct, born only to be caught and destroyed" (2 Peter 2:12). Make no mistake. The punishment that Paul speaks of is everlasting, not temporary. Moreover, the plain sense of being shut out from the presence of the Lord implies continued conscious existence.

Finally, to make the case for a second chance after death, Bell appeals to reformer Martin Luther. After belittling those who believe that the unsaved will experience "eternal conscious torment" (i.e. "not only will these 'unsaved' be punished forever, but they will be fully aware of it— in case we were concerned they might down an Ambien or two when God wasn't looking"[13]), Bell alludes to those, like Luther, who "insist that there must be some kind of 'second chance' for those who don't believe in Jesus in this lifetime." So as to leave no doubt, Bell quotes the following phrase from Luther's 1522 letter to Hans von Rechenberg: "Who would doubt God's ability to do that?"[14]

This, of course, is a powerful argument, one not easily dispensed with. For Luther to believe, no—"*insist* that there must be some kind of '*second chance*' for those who do not believe in Jesus in this life-time" must surely give the rest of us pause. Luther was no ordinary churchman; he was arguably the greatest reformer in church history. The very man who in 1517 nailed the now-famous Ninety-Five Theses to the door of the Castle Church at Wittenberg. The monk who when asked to recant famously responded, "My conscience is captive to the

Word of God. . . . Here I stand. I cannot do otherwise. May God help me."[15] Yet scarcely five years later, in his letter to Hans von Rechenberg, Luther insisted on the gospel of the second chance? Who would have thought?

If virtually anyone other than Bell said such a thing they would have been laughed out of school. But at the time, Bell was a highly acclaimed pastor, thought to be "a central figure for his generation and for the way that evangelicals are likely to do church in the next twenty years."[16] A prophetic voice writing in a book proclaimed to be a "prophetic master-piece."[17] Surely he would not gratuitously distort the life and legacy of a reformer? Or would he?

In an age in which Internet lies travel halfway around the world before truth has had the chance to put its boots on, we would do well to heed the admonition of the Apostle to the Gentiles: "Test everything. Hold on to the good" (1 Thessalonians 5:21). In doing so, we would discover that Bell has omitted Luther's *very next sentence*. A sentence forever exonerating Luther from belief in the gospel of a second chance after death. A sentence that simply reads, *"No one, however, can prove that he does do this."*[18] Moreover, anyone who has taken the time to read Luther's letter knows full well that what Bell has ascribed to him could not be further from the truth. With multitudes throughout church history, Luther was committed to the biblical belief that "man is destined to die once and after that to face judgment" (Hebrews 9:27).

C. S. Lewis was right when he wrote, "I would pay any price to be able to say truthfully 'All will be saved.' But my reason retorts, 'Without their will, or with it?' If I say 'Without their will' I at once perceive a contradiction; how can the supreme voluntary act of self-surrender be involuntary? If I say 'With their will' my reason replies, 'How if they *will not* give in?'"[19] As Lewis wisely conceded, "There are only two kinds of people in the end: those who say to God, 'Thy will be done,' and those to whom God says, in the end, *'Thy* will be done.' All that are in Hell, choose it. Without that self-choice there could be no Hell. No soul that seriously and constantly desires joy will ever miss it. Those who seek find. To those who knock it is opened."[20]

In the end, Bell's church attendee was not far off in supposing that Ghandi is destined for hell. While one might well imagine that the torment of Hitler's hell will greatly exceed that ascribed to Ghandi, in the end we can know that God is perfectly just and that all those who with knowledge and foresight spurn the grace that could have been theirs will suffer exactly what they deserve. If Ghandi considered Christ and chose to reject him, as the historical record supposes he did, then Ghandi is forever separated from God's goodness and grace. To believe otherwise reduces Christianity to sheer madness. Without choice, heaven would not be heaven; heaven would be hell. The righteous would inherit a counterfeit heaven and the unrighteous would be incarcerated in heaven against their wills. Existence in hell respects the intrinsic value and autonomy of human beings.

In sum, neither our Lord nor Luther taught anything other than hell's irrevocable reality. To distort the teachings of Luther is one thing; to distort those of our Lord, quite another.

DON'T ALL RELIGIONS LEAD TO HEAVEN?

The soul of religion is one, but it is encased in a multitude of forms.
—MAHATMA GANDHI

Before answering the question of whether all religions lead to heaven, a word of warning is in order. If you answer in the negative, you may well be ostracized for being narrow-minded and intolerant. Truth, however, is of primary concern. Thus, despite being politically incorrect, it is important to underscore the reality that it is both incorrect and illogical to maintain that all religions lead to an eternal relationship with God.

First, when you begin to examine world religions such as Judaism,

Hinduism, and Buddhism, you will immediately recognize that they directly contradict one another. For example, Moses taught that there was only one path to God, Krishna believed in many paths, and Buddha was agnostic. Logically, they can all be wrong but they can't all be right.

Furthermore, the road of religion leads steeply uphill, while the road of Christianity descends downward. Put another way, religion is fallen humanity's attempt to reach up and become acceptable to God through what we do. Christianity, on the other hand, is based on what Christ has done. He lived the perfect life we could never live and offers us his perfection as an absolutely free gift.

Finally, Jesus taught that there was only one way to eternal life. "I am the way and the truth and the life," said Jesus. "No one comes to the Father except through me" (John 14:6). Moreover, Jesus validated his claim through the immutable fact of his resurrection. The opinions of all other religious leaders are equally valid in that they are equally worthless. They died and are still dead. Only Jesus had the power to lay down his life and to take it up again. Thus, his opinion is infinitely more valid than any other.

WHAT HAPPENS TO A PERSON WHO HAS NEVER HEARD OF JESUS?

Someone asked will the heathen who have never heard the Gospel be saved? It is more a question with me whether we—who have the Gospel and fail to give it to those who have not—can be saved.
—CHARLES HADDON SPURGEON

One of the most frequently asked questions on the *Bible Answer Man* broadcast is, "What happens to those who have never heard of Jesus?" Will God condemn people to hell for not believing in someone they have never heard of?

First, people are not condemned to hell for not believing in Jesus. Rather they are already condemned because of their sin. Thus, the real question is not how can God send someone to hell, but how can God condescend to save any one of us? As Paul has so beautifully written in the book of Romans, "God demonstrates his own love for us in this: While we were still sinners, Christ died for us. Since we have now been justified by his blood, how much more shall we be saved from God's wrath" (5:8–9).

Furthermore, if ignorance were a ticket to heaven, the greatest evangelistic enterprise would not be a Billy Graham crusade but a concerted cover-up campaign. Such a campaign would focus on ending evangelism, burning Bibles, and closing churches. Soon no one would have heard of Christ and everyone would be on their way to heaven. This argument, popularly referred to as the *argumentum ad absurdum*, or the argument to a logical absurdity, underscores the reality that a claim to ignorance is hardly a ticket to heaven. Only if one is *truly* blind would they be absolved of sin (John 9:41).

Finally, it is hard to claim genuine blindness in light of creation and conscience. God is not capricious! If we respond to the light he will give us more light. In the words of the apostle Paul, "From one man he made every nation of men, that they should inhabit the whole earth; and he determined the times set for them and the exact places where they should live. God did this so that men would seek him and perhaps reach out for him and find him, though he is not far from each one of us" (Acts 17:26–27).

HOW DOES THE BIBLE DEFINE DEATH?

He who does not prepare for death is more than an ordinary fool, he is a madman.

— CHARLES HADDON SPURGEON

We think of death as the grim reaper—a despicable despot who preys on young and old alike. Sometimes death arrives suddenly; at other times it slowly sabotages the life of its victims. But biblically there is much more to death than the dissolution of this earthly body. The Bible speaks of even more horrifying realities. In addition to *somatic death* (bodily death), Scripture unveils the horrors of *spiritual death* and ultimately of the *second death*.

First, the Bible defines *somatic death*—the separation of body (*soma*) and spirit. Adam, of course, is the prototypical example. "God commanded the man, 'you are free to eat from any tree in the garden; but you must not eat from the tree of the knowledge of good and evil, for when you eat of it you will surely die'" (Genesis 2:16–17). In direct contradiction of the sovereign God the serpent said to Eve, "You will not surely die" (Genesis 3:4). And so the parents of posterity fell into lives of constant sin terminate by death. "For dust you are and to dust you will return" (Genesis 3:19). From that day to the present, somatic death has been a biological reality. Until Jesus appears a second time, the death rate will continue at one per person.

Furthermore, the Bible describes *spiritual death*. When Adam sinned, he did not immediately experience physical death; however, he did die spiritually. Thus, his sin not only initiated the looming specter of physical death, but it also ignited the actuality of spiritual death. As such, the deeper death instituted by sin is spiritual. In other words, whereas physical death separates the body from the soul, spiritual death separates the soul from God. To be spiritually separated from God, explains the apostle Paul, is to be dead in "transgressions and sins" (Ephesians 2:1) and therefore "by nature objects of wrath" (v. 3). "But because of his great love for us, God, who is rich in mercy, made us alive with Christ even when we were dead in transgressions" (vv. 4–5). "For it is by grace you have been saved, through faith—and this not from yourselves, it is the gift of God—not by works, so that no one can boast" (vv. 8–9).

Finally, there is ultimate death—what the Bible describes as the *second death*. The first death involves the death of both body and soul. This first death we may escape through our being raised spiritually with Christ in the heavenly realms (Ephesians 2:6) and finally our bodily resurrection (1 Corinthians 15). The second death, however, is inescapable. Therefore, says Jesus, "Do not be afraid of those who kill the body but cannot kill the soul. Rather, be afraid of the One who can destroy both soul and body in hell" (Matthew 10:28). Hell *is* the second death, variously described as blackest darkness forever, the lake of fire, or the fiery lake of burning sulfur. The ghastly realities of the second death are made vivid in John's vision on the island of Patmos: "If anyone's name was not found written in the book of life, he was thrown into the lake of fire" (Revelation 20:15). But "he who overcomes will not be hurt at all by the second death" (2:11).

In sum, we escape *somatic death* through the resurrection of the body, *spiritual death* by being raised up with Christ in the heavenly realms, and the *second death* by having our names "written in the Lamb's book of life" (Revelation 21:27). "But the cowardly, the unbelieving, the vile, the murderers, the sexually immoral, those who practice magic arts, the idolaters and all liars—their place will be in the fiery lake of burning sulfur. This is the second death" (v. 8).

SHOULD CHRISTIANS FEAR DEATH?

Men fear death as children fear to go in the dark.

—Francis Bacon

The tree of the knowledge of good and evil is a prime example of physical reality highlighting spiritual truth. God placed it in the middle of the garden of Eden as a test; Satan perverted it as a temptation. In eating from the tree about which God said, "When you eat of it *you will surely die*," the father of humanity actualized the specter of death (Genesis

2:17). This specter has been part of the human condition from that time until the present. In place of fearing death, however, the Christian worldview provides a realistic perspective on death and a way to overcome the fear of dying through resurrection and through relationship.

First, unlike contemporary culture, the Christian perspective on death is eminently *realistic*. Postmodernity seeks to deny death by driving it into the closet, trivialize it by treating it irreverently, or circumvent it through the use of clever clichés. Cultural thanatologists (those who study death) go as far as to view death as a friend. Christian theology, however, provides a more realistic perspective. Death is the enemy. It is the unnatural rending of the body from the soul, and as such should be regarded as a curse (Genesis 3:19; Romans 6:23). God himself emphasized this truth by relegating corpses to the class of unclean things in the purity laws set forth for the Israelites (Numbers 19:11–22). This would have impressed on the minds of ancient Hebrews the unnatural quality of death and the direct relationship between death and sin.

In like fashion, Christians today should never allow conformity to the culture to cause them to become callous toward death. Rather death should ever remain a reminder of the consequences of sin. As the apostle Paul explains, "Sin entered the world through one man, and death through sin, and in this way death came to all men" (Romans 5:12). Nonetheless, believers look forward realistically to a time in which the Lord Almighty "will swallow up death forever." A day in which the "Sovereign LORD will wipe away the tears from all faces" (Isaiah 25:8). The apostle John looked into the future and saw that very day. A day in which "there will be no more death or mourning, or crying or pain, for the old order of things has passed away" (Revelation 21:4).

Furthermore, while Christianity does not give us "a peaceful way to come to terms with death," it does give us something far greater—"a way to overcome death," through the power of *resurrection*.[21] Put another way, the promise of resurrection quells the fear of death. By viewing death with eternity in mind, Christians no longer "grieve like the rest of men, who have no hope. We believe that Jesus died and rose again and so we believe that God will bring with Jesus those who have fallen asleep in him" (1 Thessalonians 4:13). Without the resurrection of Christ, of course, there would be no such hope. Says Paul, "If the dead are not raised, then Christ has not been raised either. And if Christ has not been raised, your faith is futile; you are still in your sins. Then those also who have fallen asleep in Christ are lost. If only for this life we have hope in Christ, we are to be pitied more than all men. But Christ has indeed been raised from the dead, the firstfruits of those who have fallen asleep" (1 Corinthians 15:16–20).

Assured by the bodily resurrection of Jesus Christ, Christians may know with certainty that they too will one day be raised to live with him for all eternity (1 Corinthians 6:14). Thus, believers can realistically acknowledge the evil of death yet exude, "'O death, where is your victory? O death, where is your sting?'" (1 Corinthians 15:55 ESV; cf. Hosea 13:14). As the writer of Hebrews makes plain, Christ through his death on the cross and subsequent resurrection has forever freed Christians from the fear of death. Since the children of God "have flesh and blood, he too shared in their humanity so that by his death he might destroy him who holds the power of death—that is the devil—and free those who all their lives were held in slavery by their *fear of death*" (Hebrews 2:14–15). While Christians still die, their deaths spell freedom, not fear. "I am convinced," said Paul, "that neither death nor life, neither angels nor demons, neither the present nor the future, nor any powers, neither height nor depth, nor anything else in all creation, will be able to separate us from the love of God that is in Christ Jesus our Lord" (Romans 8:38–39).

Finally, just as the metaphysical reality of death is removed through the reality of resurrection, the psychological reality of death is relieved through the deepening of relationship between those who are redeemed and their Redeemer. Put another way, an ever-deepening *relationship* with

Christ is the key to overcoming the psychological fear of death. This is the very thing I witnessed in my father as he breathed his last. He had spent a lifetime deepening his relationship with God and in the end transitioned peacefully into the loving presence of his heavenly Father. Relationship, likewise, is what Paul was driving at when writing, "For to me, to live is Christ and to die is gain" (Philippians 1:21). So passionate was Paul respecting his relationship to the Redeemer that he was mentally torn between the prospect of living and dying. In fact, that is precisely how he put it: "If I am to go on living in the body, this will mean fruitful labor for me. Yet what shall I choose? I do not know! *I am torn between the two*: I desire to depart and be with Christ, which is better by far; but it is more necessary for you that I remain in the body" (Philippians 1:22–24).

In sum, believers throughout the ages have viewed death realistically. On the one hand, death is viewed as the enemy—an enduring reminder of the consequences of sin. On the other, it is viewed as a foe defeated through resurrection and an ever-deepening relationship with Christ, who is "the firstfruits of those who have fallen asleep" (1 Corinthians 15:20). With the reality of death, we can look forward to the resurrection and an enduring relationship with the lover of our souls.

DOES SUICIDE PREVENT PEOPLE FROM GOING TO HEAVEN?

Obviously a suicide is the opposite of a martyr. A martyr is a man who cares so much for something outside him, that he forgets his own personal life. A suicide is a man who cares so little for anything outside him, that he wants to see the last of everything. One wants something to begin: the other wants everything to end.

—G. K. CHESTERTON

In a society of stressed-out people, suicide is not a singularly secular dilemma. Nor is it relegated to any particular segment of society. It is a plague infecting rich and poor; famous and infamous; young and old. Biblically, the Old Testament Saul and the New Testament Judas both committed suicide. And today, suicide is said to be the third leading cause of death among young people ages fifteen to twenty-four.[22] As the incidence of suicide continues to skyrocket, I am asked with ever-increasing frequency whether suicide is an unforgivable sin.

First, we should note that no single act is unforgivable. Peter did the unthinkable: three times he denied his Lord with vile oaths. Yet Christ not only forgave Peter, but his confession, "You are the Christ, the Son of the living God" (Matthew 16:16), became the cornerstone of the Christian faith. The Bible consistently teaches that those who spend eternity separated from God do so because they willingly, knowingly, and continuously reject the forgiveness that could be theirs. The apostle John refers to this as the "sin that leads to death" (1 John 5:16) in that those who refuse forgiveness through Christ will spend eternity separated from his grace and love. Conversely, those who sincerely desire forgiveness can be absolutely certain that God will never spurn them. Thus, while saints in a state of despondency and depression have done the unthinkable, no one can say with certainty that they are precluded from inheriting eternal life.

Furthermore, it is crucial to note that suicide is the murder of oneself. Because you and I are made in the image of God, to murder oneself is to show contempt for the crowning jewel of God's creation and, even more seriously, to show contempt for the Creator himself. We must ever be mindful of the reality that suicide is a direct attack on the sovereignty of the very One who knit us together in our mother's womb. As the psalmist so eloquently elucidates, "You created my inmost being; you knit me together in my mother's womb. I praise you because I am fearfully and wonderfully made; your works are wonderful, I know that full well. My frame was not hidden from you when I was made in the secret place. When I was woven together in the depths of the earth, your eyes saw my unformed body. All the days ordained for me are written in your book before one of them came to be" (Psalm 139:13–16).

Finally, while suicide is not an unforgivable sin, those who take the sacred name of Christ upon their lips dare not contemplate it. Our lives belong to God and he alone has the prerogative to bring them to an end. In the words of the Almighty, "See now that I myself am he! There is no god beside me. I put to death and bring to life, I have wounded and I heal, and no one can deliver out of my hand" (Deuteronomy 32:39). In the deepest valleys of life, we must remember that though we walk in the midst of difficulties, it is God who preserves our lives. Says David, "The Lord will fulfill his purpose for me; your love, O Lord, endures forever—do not abandon the works of your hands" (Psalm 138:8).

In short, while suicide is a direct violation of the sixth commandment—"you shall not murder" (Exodus 20:13; cf. Genesis 9:6)—it is not an unforgivable sin. Nonetheless, those who are created in the image of God must never contemplate taking for themselves a prerogative that is God's alone.

CHAPTER
TEN

⋮

Is there really a resurrection?

HOW CAN WE BE SURE ABOUT THE RESURRECTION OF CHRIST?

I know the resurrection is a fact, and Watergate proved it to me. How?
Because 12 men testified they had seen Jesus raised from the dead,
then they proclaimed that truth for 40 years, never once denying it.
Every one was beaten, tortured, stoned and put in prison. They would
not have endured that if it weren't true. Watergate embroiled 12 of
the most powerful men in the world—and they couldn't keep a lie for
three weeks. You're telling me 12 apostles could keep a lie for 40 years?
Absolutely impossible.

—CHARLES COLSON

If devotees of the kingdom of the cults, adherents of world religions, or liberal scholars are correct, the biblical account of the resurrection of Christ is fiction, fantasy, or a gargantuan fraud. If, on the other hand, Christianity is factually reliable, his resurrection is the greatest feat in human history. No middle ground exists. The resurrection is history or hoax, miracle or myth, fact or fantasy.

First, liberal and conservative scholars alike agree that the body of Jesus was buried in the private tomb of Joseph of Arimathea. As a member of the Jewish court that convicted Jesus, Joseph of Arimathea is unlikely to be Christian fiction. Jesus' burial in the tomb of Joseph of Arimathea is substantiated by Mark's gospel and is, therefore, far too early to have been the subject of legendary corruption. The earliest Jewish response to the resurrection of Christ presupposes the empty tomb; and in the centuries following the resurrection, the fact of the empty tomb was forwarded by Jesus' friends and foes alike.[1]

Additionally, as philosopher and apologist William Lane Craig points out, "when you understand the role of women in first-century Jewish society, what's really extraordinary is that this empty tomb story should feature women as the discoverers of the empty tomb in the first place."

Craig concludes, "The fact that women are the first witnesses to the empty tomb is most plausibly explained by the reality that—like it or not—they *were* the discoverers of the empty tomb! This shows that the gospel writers faithfully recorded what happened, even if it was embarrassing. This bespeaks the historicity of this tradition rather than its legendary status."[2]

Furthermore, Jesus gave his disciples many convincing proofs that he had risen from the dead. Paul, for example, points out that Christ appeared to many people on many occasions. First "he appeared to Peter and then to the Twelve. After that he appeared to more than five hundred of the brothers at the same time, most of whom are still living, though some have fallen asleep. Then he appeared to James, then to all the apostles, and last of all he appeared to me also, as to one abnormally born" (1 Corinthians 15:5–8).

It would have been one thing to attribute these supernatural experiences to people who had already died. It was quite another to attribute them to multitudes who were still alive. As famed New Testament scholar C. H. Dodd points out, "There can hardly be any purpose in mentioning the fact that most of the 500 are still alive, unless Paul is saying, in effect, 'The witnesses are there to be questioned.'"[3]

Finally, what happened as a result of the resurrection is unprecedented in human history. In the span of a few hundred years, a small band of seemingly insignificant believers succeeded in turning an entire empire upside down. While it is conceivable that they would have faced torture, vilification, and even cruel deaths for what they fervently believed to be true, it is inconceivable that they would have been willing to die for what they knew to be a lie. As Dr. Simon Greenleaf, the famous Royall Professor of Law at Harvard, put it, "If it were morally possible for them to have been deceived in this matter, every human motive operated to lead them to discover and avow their error. . . . If then their testimony was not true, there was no possible motive for this fabrication."[4]

WHAT ARE SOME OF THE BIBLE'S RESURRECTION PROMISES?

Christianity does not offer a peaceful way to come to terms with death. No, it offers instead a way to overcome death. Christ stands for Life, and His resurrection should give convincing proof that God is not satisfied with any "cycle of life" that ends in death. He will go to any extent—he did go to any extent—to break that cycle.

—PHILLIP YANCEY

From the moment we are born, our bodies begin sowing the seeds of biological destruction. Yet for Christians death is hardly the end. The cycle of life and death is forever broken through resurrection. Four days after Lazarus died, Jesus said to Martha, "Your brother will rise again. Martha answered, 'I know he will rise again in the resurrection at the last day.' Jesus said to her, 'I am the resurrection and the life. He who believes in me will live, even though he dies; and whoever lives and believes in me will never die'" (John 11:23–26). In saying this Jesus pointed to himself as the very one who would overcome death and the grave and as such ensure that all who put their trust in him would experience resurrection—as promised by Jesus and the prophets.

First, we should note that the most significant promise of resurrection comes from Jesus Christ himself. When the Jews demanded that he prove his authority over temple, priest, and sacrifice, Jesus responded, "Destroy this temple and I will raise it again in three days" (John 2:19). The Jews thought he was speaking of Herod's temple, which had taken forty-six years to build. "But the temple he had spoken of was his body" (v. 21).

Context here is crucial. Jesus had just "made a whip out of cords and drove all from the temple area, both sheep and cattle; he scattered the coins of the money changers and overturned their tables. To those who sold doves he said, 'Get these out of here! How dare you turn my

Father's house into a market!'" (John 2:15–16). The meaning was not lost on his disciples. They had seen his miracles. They knew who he was and remembered the prophetic words of King David: "Zeal for your house will consume me" (v. 17).

The Jewish Sanhedrin also knew of the miracles of Jesus. Thus, they did not immediately instruct the temple police to arrest him for civil disobedience. Instead they asked for a miracle: "What miraculous sign can you show us to prove your authority to do all this?" (John 2:18). In place of a sign, Jesus presented a prophecy. Not just *a* prophecy—*the* prophecy. The prophecy demonstrating that the whole of the Law and the Prophets pointed forward to him. The prophecy signifying that the Word of God cannot be broken. The prophetic star shining most brightly in the constellation of biblical prophecy. "Destroy this temple," said Jesus, "and I will raise it again in three days" (v. 19).

When Jesus uttered the words "destroy this temple," he was standing in the shadow of a sanctuary of which he himself was the substance. Instead of bowing to the substance, the temple keepers reveled in its shadow. "It has taken forty-six years to build this temple," they sneered, "and you are going to raise it in three days?" (John 2:20). Enamored by the picture, they were oblivious to the Person. Sadly, they loved the type and loathed the antitype who had emerged in their midst through the doorway of Old Testament prophesies.

Jesus made his typological relationship to the earthly sanctuary explicit when he pronounced, "One greater than the temple is here" (Matthew 12:6). In saying this he pointed to himself as the antitypical fulfillment of all that had been spoken by Moses and the prophets. "After he was raised from the dead, the disciples recalled what he had said. *Then they believed the Scripture and the words that Jesus had spoken*" (John 2:22). Truly, the glorious fulfillment of Christ's prophesied resurrection from the dead—"Destroy this temple and I will raise it again in three days"—is the prophetic star illumining the reality that Christians too will be resurrected.

Furthermore, a starry host of resurrection prophecies banishes the darkness of unbelief and doubt. Daniel likens the resurrection of saints to the glory of the stars: "Multitudes who sleep in the dust of the earth will awake; some to everlasting life, others to shame and everlasting contempt. Those who are wise will shine like the brightness of the heavens, and those who lead many to righteousness, like the stars for ever and ever" (Daniel 12:2–3). The resurrection envisioned is clear and unambiguous. Daniel speaks here not of the disembodied state that follows death but of the bodily resurrection that follows the disembodied state. The martyrs were not promised a mere resuscitation but a majestic resurrection in a new order of things in which they would shine like stars. The rock cut out, but not by human hands, "will set up a kingdom that will never be destroyed, nor will it be left to another people. It will crush all those kingdoms and bring them to an end, but it will itself endure forever" (Daniel 2:44). The resurrection prophesied by Daniel has not yet been fulfilled.

Isaiah, likewise, looks to the resurrection of "a man of sorrows and familiar with suffering" (Isaiah 53:3), as the earnest of our resurrection on the last day. "After the suffering of his soul," exudes Isaiah, "he will see the light of life and be satisfied" (Isaiah 53:11). In like fashion, our bodies will be resurrected from the dust of the ground. The mortal will be clothed with immortality. Isaiah's prophecy is pregnant with the promise of new birth: "Your dead will live; their bodies will rise. You who dwell in the dust, wake up and shout for joy. Your dew is like the dew of the morning; the earth will give birth to her dead" (Isaiah 26:19). It is from the dust that God created humankind; it is to the dust humankind returns; yet it is also from the dust that our DNA emerges as the pattern for resurrected bodies. The restoration of Israel points forward to the restoration of true Israel, and the restoration of true Israel is the earnest of every individual who realizes in Immanuel the promise of resurrection from the dead.

The typological relationship between the resuscitation of Israel and the resurrection of true Israel is seen with stunning clarity in Ezekiel's vision of dry bones scattered in a valley. Dry and discarded, the bones were in danger of disintegrating into dust. A poignant picture of the people of the promise—wasted and dead in exile and sin. Ezekiel prophesied as he was commanded by God and suddenly "there was a noise, a rattling sound, and the bones came together, bone to bone. I looked," said Ezekiel, "and tendons and flesh appeared on them and skin covered them, but there was no breath in them" (37:7). Again Ezekiel prophesied as he was commanded, and breath entered the bodies; "they came to life and stood up on their feet—a vast army" (v. 10).

The interpretation leaves little to the imagination. God would open the graves and restore Israel. "I will put my Spirit in you and you will live, and I will settle you in your own land. Then you will know that I the LORD have spoken, and I have done it, declares the LORD" (Ezekiel 37:14). The resurrection of Israel to the land, of course, is but a type of resurrection that finds ultimate fulfillment in the resurrection of the Lord—who is the locus of the land. As such, the resurrection imagery of Ezekiel finds ultimate resolution in the resurrection of Christ and the resurrection of Christians. The antitype that fulfills the entire mosaic of Old Testament resurrection prophecies left no doubt about this coming resurrection: "Do not be amazed at this, for a time is coming when all who are in their graves will hear his voice and come out—those who have done good will rise to live, and those who have done evil will rise to be condemned" (John 5:28–29). If Christ had not himself been resurrected, the promise that he will resurrect dry bones in scattered graves would be as empty as the tomb guaranteeing its fulfillment.

Finally, among the Old Testament resurrection prophecies, the Star of David prophecy is most brilliant of all. I refer neither to the Israeli flag nor to a badge of shame forced on Jews during the Holocaust, but to a bright and morning star in the resurrection prophecies of David. In the first apostolic sermon recorded in the New Testament, Peter zeroed in on this prophecy. Addressing God-fearing Jews and converts to Judaism from every nation under heaven, he spoke of their culpability in the death of Jesus. "This man was handed over to you by God's set purpose and foreknowledge; and you, with the help of wicked men, put him to death by nailing him to the cross. But God raised him from the dead, freeing him from the agony of death, because it was impossible for death to keep its hold on him" (Acts 2:23–24).

To prove that the death of Christ was in accordance with God's set purpose and foreknowledge—so that sin, the root cause of death, might be atoned for—Peter quoted the Star of David prophecy: "I have set the Lord always before me. Because he is at my right hand, I will not be shaken. Therefore my heart is glad and my tongue rejoices; my body also will rest secure, *because you will not abandon me to the grave, nor will you let your Holy One see decay.* You have made known to me the path of life; you will fill me with joy in your presence, with eternal pleasures at your right hand" (Psalm 16:8–11).

Peter left no doubt that David's words were a direct prophecy regarding the resurrection of Jesus. "I can tell you confidently that the patriarch David died and was buried, and his tomb is here to this day. But he was a prophet and knew that God had promised him on oath that he would place one of his descendants on his throne. Seeing what was ahead, he spoke of the resurrection of the Christ, that he was not abandoned to the grave, nor did his body see decay. God has raised this Jesus to life, and we are all witnesses of the fact" (Acts 2:29–32). Peter's Pentecost sermon was so persuasive—so powerful, so poignant—that despite not having so much as a microphone, three thousand were added to the church that very day.

The apostle Paul, likewise, highlighted the Star of David prophecy as powerful proof that what God had promised a thousand years earlier through the quintessential king of Israel was fulfilled by the resurrection of Christ. On the Sabbath, this persecutor-turned-proselytizer had entered the synagogue in Antioch. The synagogue rulers invited him to speak. Standing up, he spoke of God's providence in raising up Israel as the means through which the message of salvation would be spread throughout the earth. Tragically, the rulers of Jerusalem had not recognized Messiah in their midst. "Though they found no proper ground for a death sentence, they asked Pilate to have him executed. When they had carried out all that was written about him, they took him down from the tree and laid him in a tomb. But God raised him from the dead" (Acts 13:28–30).

This resurrection was not only the fulfillment of a prophecy, but it was an utterly unique event in the whole of recorded history. Others might have been resuscitated, but their bodies were even now experiencing decomposition and decay. Jesus, however, was resurrected, never to decay. "What God promised our fathers," said Paul, "he has fulfilled for us, their children, by raising up Jesus" (Acts 13:32–33). In evidence, Paul quoted the words of the familiar psalm—words no doubt emblazoned upon the hearts of his hearers: *"You will not let your Holy One see decay"* (Psalm 16:10). Such words, said Paul, were obviously not fulfilled in the death of David. "For when David had served God's purpose in his own generation, he fell asleep; he was buried with his fathers and his body decayed. But the one whom God raised from the dead did not see decay" (Acts 13:36–37).

As with Peter, Paul's sermon struck with combustible force. "On the next Sabbath almost the whole city gathered to hear the word of the Lord" (v. 44). The fallout was predictable. "When the Jews saw the crowds, they were filled with jealousy and talked abusively against what Paul was saying" (v. 45). However, when the Gentiles heard, "they were glad and honored the word of the Lord; and all who were appointed for eternal life believed" (v. 48). As a result, "the word of the Lord spread through the whole region" (v. 49).

As it did two thousand years ago, the Star of David prophecy continues to pierce the hearts of the open-minded. Paul made clear in his sermon that the resurrection of Jesus Christ was not without witness: "For many days he was seen by those who had traveled with him from Galilee to Jerusalem. They are now his witnesses" (Acts 13:31). In the span of a few hundred years, the small band of witnesses that had traveled with the Messiah succeeded in turning the Caesar cult upside down. Why? Because they were utterly convinced that, like their Master, they would one day rise from the grave in glorified, resurrected bodies. Thus, as one after another was put to a terrifying death, those who survived pressed on, resilient, resolute, rejoicing.

The conclusion of the matter is this: Jesus said, "I am the resurrection and the life. He who believes in me will live, even though he dies; and whoever lives and believes in me will never die" (John 11:25–26). All who put their trust in Jesus can be absolutely certain that they will experience resurrection. Jesus promised that he would lay down his life and take it up again in three days. His fulfillment of the promise is the guarantee that there is life *after* life-after-life. There is life after life, in that the redeemed continue to exist in the presence of the Redeemer. There is life *after* life-after-life, in that just as Jesus rose bodily from the grave, so too our bodies will rise immortal, imperishable, and incorruptible (1 Corinthians 15:50–56). Proof of the resurrection is so certain that millions have willingly laid down their lives, certain that they will take them up again. You can be just as certain. For all who are in Christ, the resurrection awaits.

CAN THE CREMATED BE RESURRECTED?

Forasmuch as it hath pleased Almighty God of his great mercy to take unto himself the soul of our dear brother here departed, we therefore commit his body to the ground; earth to earth, ashes to ashes, dust to dust; in sure and certain hope of the Resurrection to eternal life, through our Lord Jesus Christ; who shall change our vile body, that it may be like unto his glorious body, according to the mighty working, whereby he is able to subdue all things to himself.

—BOOK OF COMMON PRAYER

Cremation has become an increasingly popular means for disposing of the dead. In Japan virtually everyone makes ashes of themselves, and in America it is now estimated that within the next decade the majority will choose cremation over burial.[5] Most cite emotional, economic, or ecological reasons. Emotionally, cremation is thought to bring immediate closure to the grieving process—though in reality the opposite appears to be the case. Economically, cremation is less costly than burial —however, eternal values must always take precedence over economic considerations. Ecologically, with rare exception, there is no deficit of suitable burial lands. While the cremated can most certainly be resurrected, unlike burial, cremation does not provide an object lesson for resurrection.

First, burial symbolizes the promise of resurrection by anticipating the preservation of the body. In an age of growing biblical illiteracy, it is increasingly important to highlight physical resurrection as the centerpiece of the biblical worldview. Contrarily, cremation better symbolizes the pagan worldview of reincarnation or escape from the body. Thus, in sharp contrast to reincarnationists, who look forward to being relieved of their bodies, resurrectionists look forward to the restoration of their bodies.

The caterpillar again provides the perfect illustration. Far from being reincarnated as a cockatoo, the caterpillar is physically transformed into a beautiful butterfly. The chrysalis is, as it were, its casket. There constituent parts of the caterpillar are transformed and in time a beautiful butterfly soars into the heavens. While the caterpillar and the butterfly are the same physically, they are clearly no longer the same organizationally.

Furthermore, Scripture clearly favors burial over cremation. The Old Testament pattern was always burial except in highly unusual circumstances. The exception that best proves the rule is the partial cremation of King Saul and his sons—and even in this case, the bodies were burned, but the bones were buried (1 Samuel 31:12–13).

Likewise, the New Testament pattern is always burial. Indeed, the apostle Paul includes burial as an essential part of the gospel in his first letter to the Corinthians. "For what I received I passed on to you as of first importance: that Christ died for our sins according to the Scriptures, *that he was buried,* that he was raised on the third day according to the Scriptures" (1 Corinthians 15:3–4). Likewise, Paul equates baptism with both burial and resurrection when he reminds Roman readers that they were buried with Christ through baptism into death "in order that, just as Christ was raised from the dead through the glory of the Father, we too might live a new life" (6:4).

Finally, burial highlights the sanctity of the body. In the Christian worldview, the body is significant not only because we were created in the imago Dei but also because there is numerical identity between the body that dies and the body that is resurrected. While resurrection does not necessitate that every atom is resuscitated, it does require continuity between our present bodies and the permanent bodies that will be.

DNA is an apt illustration. Just as your DNA is the pattern for your present body, so too it is the pattern for the body that will be. Your present body developed in a cursed creation, but not so your permanent body. It will flower to complete perfection and will never experience devolution. Indeed, the glorious promise of Christianity is that when Jesus Christ appears a second time our souls will return to glorified bodies that will never age and will forever be vibrant. That is our hope. That is our destiny.

In sum, while burial points to resurrection, cremation in its Eastern permutations highlights escape from the body. Nonetheless, while cremation does not point to the resurrection of God, God has no problem resurrecting the cremated.

WILL ANGELS EVER REBEL AGAIN?

Angels have a much more important place in the Bible than the devil and his demons.

—BILLY GRAHAM

The question of whether the angels could rebel again presents a conundrum of sorts. If we suggest that angels are not free to sin in the present, we are simultaneously suggesting they are not actually free at all. If on the other hand we say that holy angels are free to sin in the present just as fallen angels were free to sin in the past we thereby suggest they are not presently actualized in their choice not to sin. Thus the question is, how can we know for certain that angels will not rebel again?

First, we may answer this question by simply stating that this is what the Scriptures say. Scripture knows nothing of a future rebellion of the holy angels. Moreover, in eternity there is no place for sin. Says the apostle John, "Nothing impure will ever enter the New Jerusalem, nor will anyone who does what is shameful and deceitful but only those whose names are written in the Lamb's book of life" (Revelation 21:27).

Furthermore, we can know that the angels will not rebel a second time in that they passed the supreme test the first time. If ever there was a time for the angelic hosts, replete in requisite knowledge, to have rebelled against the Sovereign of creation it would have been when Lucifer, "the Guardian Cherub," "Morning Star," "Son of the Dawn," proud in splendor and wisdom, seduced a third of the angels to follow him in rebellion (Revelation 12:4).

Finally, to contend that the holy angels are free yet not able to sin is hardly contradictory. God himself is the prime exemplar. He has ultimate freedom and yet is not able to sin. The holy angels are in much the same condition. In obedience they are not only genuinely free but have been actualized in righteousness.

DOES GOD KNOW WHO WILL BE IN HEAVEN?

I believe we can honestly affirm that the God who is "perfect in knowl-edge" (Job 37:16), the almighty God whose "understanding has no limit" (Psalm 147:5), the great God who "knows everything" (1 John 3:20) does indeed possess full and absolute and infallible knowledge of all future events—including all actions freely chosen by human beings.
—STEVEN C. ROY

There would be little need to address this question were it not for a significant movement within contemporary Christianity known as open theism—a movement that holds God does *not* have exhaustive knowl-edge of the future. Not only so, but an ever-increasing number of people suppose that if God knew the future our choices would be fatalistically determined, not free. Thus, the question is, does God know who will inherit eternal life in the new heavens and the new earth?

First, however else one seeks to resolve the tension between God's knowledge of the future and our freedom to act or act otherwise, we must readily acknowledge that the biblical writers unambiguously communicate that the knowledge of God is exhaustive. Jesus himself foreknew who would live eternally in his loving presence in that their names were written in the book of life from the creation of the world (Revelation 17:8). Moreover, he predicted that Judas would betray him (John 6:64, 70–71) and that Peter would deny him three times (Matthew 26:34, 71–75). Knowledge of the future is not only the test of a true prophet (Deuteronomy 18:22) but also the test of a true God (Isaiah 42:9, 43:9–12, 44:7, 48:3–7). The Lord says to idols, "Declare to us the things to come, tell us what the future holds, so we may know that you are gods" (41:22–23). Again, the Lord says, "I make known the end from the beginning, from ancient times, what is still to come" (46:10).

Furthermore, we should note that theologians throughout church history readily affirm that God fully knows who will and will not be in heaven on the basis of divine attributes such as *perfection* (God not only knows himself perfectly but he knows all the ways in which human beings will participate in his perfection); *infinity* (God is infinite by nature and therefore by nature knows all things past, present, future, actual, and contingent); and *eternality* (God is not bound by time and thus knows the future with the same eternal prescience with which he knows the present and the past). As Augustine aptly wrote in the *City of God*: "He comprehends all that takes place in time—the not-yet-existing future, the existing present, and the no-longer-existing past—in an immutable and eternal present."[6]

Finally, what is acknowledged in Scripture and affirmed throughout church history does not in the least nullify human freedom. Why? Because knowledge of something does not presuppose the causation of that something. By way of explanation, Augustine noted that someone may well have comprehensive knowledge of particular past events without being involved in them at all. Thus it seems plausible that God, who exists outside of time, can know our future choices without causing them. If God knows but does not cause our choices, there is no reason to suppose that such choices can't be free.

In sum, God knows the future exhaustively. As such, he knows who are and are not the inheritors of eternal life. God's knowledge of the future, however, in no way compromises, confuses, or contradicts human freedom.

CHAPTER
ELEVEN

⋮

What about the end times?

WHEN WILL THE SECOND COMING HAPPEN?

Jesus fully expected that the history of the world as we know it (well, as he knew it) was going to come to a screeching halt, that God was soon going to intervene in the affairs of this world, overthrow the forces of evil in a cosmic act of judgment, destroy huge masses of humanity, and abolish existing human political and religious institutions. All this would be a prelude to the arrival of a new order on earth, the Kingdom of God. Moreover, Jesus expected this cataclysmic end of history would come in his own generation, at least during the lifetime of his disciples. It's pretty shocking stuff, really. And the evidence that Jesus believed and taught it is fairly impressive.

—BART D. EHRMAN

Jesus began his famous Olivet Discourse by walking away from the very temple that afforded the Jewish people their spiritual and sociological significance. When the disciples called the Master's attention to the magnificence of the temple and its surroundings, he replied, "I tell you the truth, not one stone here will be left on another; every one will be thrown down" (Matthew 24:2). Filled with apocalyptic awe and anxiety, the disciples asked, "When will this happen, and what will be the sign of your coming and of the end of the age?" (Matthew 24:3). In sober response, Jesus told his disciples that they would witness his coming within a generation. So as to leave no doubt as to the time of his coming, Jesus said to his disciples, "I tell you the truth, *this generation* will certainly not pass away until all these things have happened. Heaven and earth will pass away, but my words will never pass away" (Matthew 24:34–35). Skeptics have been quick to point out that by these words, Jesus demonstrated beyond the peradventure of a doubt that he was a false prophet—for though the temple was destroyed within a generation, the second coming of Christ did not take place as prophesied.

First, let me acknowledge that when Jesus said, "*this* generation will certainly not pass away," that is precisely what he meant. Allow me to state the obvious: our Lord was not grammatically challenged in the least! Had he wanted to draw the attention of his disciples to a generation two thousand years hence, he would not have confused them with the adjective "this." There is no mysterious esoteric meaning locked up in the grammar. Indeed, the phrase "this generation" appears with surprising regularity in the Gospels, and it always applies to the contemporaries of Jesus. For example in the "seven woes" preceding the Olivet Discourse, Jesus warned the Pharisees and the teachers of the Law of the judgment *they* would experience for rejecting Messiah in their midst. While anti-Semites have delighted in assigning the judgments of Jesus to Jews in their contemporary generations, Jesus left no room for such misguided interpretations. Instead, he directly and specifically addressed his contemporaries, saying, "I tell you the truth, all this will come upon *this generation*" (Matthew 23:36). Without exception, the phrase "this generation" refers to the then-present generation—and most certainly not the twenty-first century!

Furthermore, it should be noted that skeptics are wholly misguided in supposing that when Jesus spoke of his "coming on the clouds of the sky with power and great glory" that he spoke of his *second coming*. If they understood the language of the Bible they might not be as quick to wag their fingers at the Master. When Jesus said, "They will see the Son of Man coming on the clouds of the sky, with power and great glory" (Matthew 24:30), he was using language that anyone familiar with the Old Testament would readily grasp. Recall, for example, the Old Testament passage in which Daniel sees a vision of "one like a son of man, coming with the clouds of heaven. He approached the ancient of Days and was led into his presence" (Daniel 7:13). Here "one like a son of man" is clearly not *descending* to earth in his second coming but rather *ascending* to the throne of the Almighty in vindication and exaltation. No doubt many similar passages are even now flooding through the minds of readers familiar with the Scriptures. Like Daniel, Isaiah,

Ezekiel, and a host of prophets before him, Jesus employed the language of "clouds" to warn his disciples of the judgment that would befall Jerusalem and the temple within a generation. Far from predicting his second coming, Jesus was telling his disciples that those who witnessed Jerusalem's destruction would likewise see his vindication and exaltation as Israel's rightful king.

Finally, it should be noted that when the disciples asked Jesus about "the end of the age," they were clearly not asking Jesus about the end of the world (*kosmos*). As should be obvious, they were asking Jesus about the end of the current corrupt age (*aion*) of sacrifice in the context of his chilling prediction that the temple and its buildings would be destroyed. Common sense alone should be sufficient to convince the unbiased that redefining "coming" to mean "second coming" and "end of the age" to mean "end of the world" is at best misguided. When Jesus said, "I tell *you* the truth, *this generation* will certainly not pass away until *all these things* have happened," his disciples did not for a moment think he was speaking of his second coming or of the end of the cosmos. As conflicted as they may have been about the character of Christ's kingdom or the scope of his rule, they were not in the least confused about whom he was addressing.

As Jesus was addressing a first-century audience when he spoke of the destruction of the temple, so too he was addressing his contemporaries when he spoke of his coming in judgment on Jerusalem. "The days will come upon *you* when *your* enemies will build an embankment against *you* and encircle *you* and hem *you* in on every side. They will dash *you* to the ground, *you* and the children within *your* walls. They will not leave one stone on another, because *you* did not recognize the time of God's *coming* to *you*" (Luke 19:43–44). One thing should be crystal clear to all those who read Christ's Olivet Discourse through biblical eyes: our Lord's use of the pronoun "you" throughout directly and specifically references a first-century, not a twenty-first-century, audience.

IS IT BIBLICAL TO BELIEVE IN THE RESURRECTION OF ANTICHRIST?

You marvel that I speak directly to your hearts without amplification,
yet you saw me raise myself from the dead. Who but the most high god
has power over death? Who but god controls the earth and sky?

—NICOLAE CARPATHIA

In *The Indwelling*, the seventh volume of the wildly popular Left Behind series, Nicolae Carpathia, the novel's Antichrist character, dies and is resurrected physically in order to vindicate his claim to be God. Just like Christ, Antichrist dies on a Friday and rises from the dead on the first day of the week. And just like Christ, he has Godlike power over "earth and sky."[1] Though the resurrection of Antichrist has been popularized as factually believable, we must ask whether it is actually biblical.

First, belief in the resurrection of Antichrist is driven by a woodenly literalistic interpretation of Revelation 13. Here the apostle John says the "fatal wound" of the Beast "had been healed." Based on this pretext, it is supposed that, like Christ, the Beast (Antichrist) will be empowered to lay down his life and to take it up again, thus demonstrating that he is God. What is not accounted for by this literalism is that Revelation 13 also communicates that the Beast had seven heads and only one of his seven heads "seemed" to have been fatally wounded. Moreover, the Beast is described as having had "ten horns," resembling "a leopard," having "feet like those of a bear," and boasting a "mouth like that of a lion."

Furthermore, belief in the resurrection of Antichrist erodes warrant for the resurrection and deity of our Lord and Savior Jesus Christ. Why? Because Christ was unique in the whole of human history. He—and he alone—had the power to lay down his life and to take it up again, thus demonstrating that he is God in human flesh. As such, Christ does not stand in a line of peers with Antichrist, Muhammad, or Zoroaster. In the words of the resurrected Christ: "I am the First and the Last. I am the Living One; I was dead, and behold I am alive for ever and ever! And I hold the keys of death and Hades" (Revelation 1:17–18). To suppose that Antichrist can do what Christ did is not only blasphemous but among the gravest of theological errors that can be imagined. In short, if Antichrist could rise from the dead and control the earth and sky, Christianity would lose the basis for believing that Christ's resurrection vindicated his claim to deity.

Finally, in the biblical worldview, Satan can parody the work of Christ through "all kinds of counterfeit miracles, signs and wonders" (2 Thessalonians 2:9), but he cannot perform truly miraculous signs and wonders as Christ did. The notion that Satan can perform acts that are indistinguishable from the genuine miracles of the Messiah suggests a dualistic worldview in which the Savior and Satan are equal and opposite powers competing for dominance. Indeed, if Antichrist has power over earth and sky and can realistically raise the dead, on what basis would we not worship him?

As with the sale of indulgences in medieval times, the sale of *The Indwelling* in modern times bears testimony to the reality that millions of believers have bought into pretexts and premises that are decidedly unbiblical.

DOES "COMING ON THE CLOUDS" REFER TO CHRIST'S SECOND COMING?

Jesus certainly thought that his second coming would occur in clouds of glory before the death of all the people who were living at that time.

—BERTRAND RUSSELL

Skeptics such as Bertrand Russell, Albert Schweitzer, and more recently Bart Ehrman believe Jesus to be a false prophet because he predicted his "coming on the clouds" within the lifetime of his disciples. The question is, did Jesus have the second coming in mind or does "coming on the clouds" (Matthew 24:30) have a different meaning?

First, it should be noted that when Jesus told Caiaphas and the court that condemned him to death that they would "see the Son of Man *coming on the clouds* of the sky, with power and great glory" (Matthew 24:30), he was obviously not speaking of his second coming but rather of his coming on clouds in terms of judgment on Jerusalem (Matthew 26:63–64). As Caiaphas and the court knew full well, "coming on the clouds" was an Old Testament metaphor pointing to God as sovereign judge of the nations. In the words of Isaiah, "See, the Lord rides on a swift *cloud* and is *coming* to Egypt. The idols of Egypt tremble before him, and the hearts of the Egyptians melt within them" (Isaiah 19:1). It seems obvious that coming on clouds in this context is language that denotes judgment. Why then should anyone suggest that Christ's coming on clouds in the context of the Olivet Discourse would refer to anything other than the judgment that Jerusalem would experience within a generation just as Jesus had prophesied? Inevitably we must ask ourselves whether it is credible to suppose that Jesus, heir to the linguistic legacy of the prophets, would twist their language into a literalistic labyrinth.

Furthermore, the "coming on the clouds" judgment metaphor was clearly intended for a first-century audience, not a twenty-first-century audience. As such, Jesus employed the language of "clouds" to warn his disciples of judgment that would befall Jerusalem within their generation. Using final consummation language to characterize a near-future event, the Master of metaphor prophesied that they would see "the Son of Man coming on the clouds of the sky, with power and great glory" (Matthew 24:30). Far from predicting his second coming, Jesus was telling his disciples that those who witnessed Jerusalem's destruction would likewise see his vindication as Israel's rightful king. Little wonder then that all who read Christ's Olivet Discourse—whether skeptic or seeker—immediately presume that when Jesus uses the pronoun *you*, he was quite evidently addressing a first-century audience. Thus, when someone seeks to seduce them otherwise, their baloney detectors begin blinking furiously. Indeed, the pontifications of modern-day prophecy pundits have become an obstacle to those who might otherwise be drawn to the reality of Christ. Better by far that those who love the Word and the Word made flesh learn to reach out to the lost by explaining the Old Testament context out of which words such as "coming" and "clouds" are derived.

Finally, it should be noted that Jesus' "coming on the clouds" to judge Jerusalem in the first century points forward to the end of time when he will "come again with glory to judge the quick and the dead." Jesus, in concert with prophets ranging from Isaiah in the Old Testament to John in the New, uses apocalyptic language pointing to final-future realities to describe judgment in his generation. While the near-future catastrophes fulfill the cosmic language, they most certainly do not exhaust their meaning. Indeed, as Peter's apocalyptic prophecy of judgment on Jerusalem suggests, a day of ultimate judgment looms on the horizon. "The heavens will disappear with a roar; the elements will be destroyed by fire, and the earth and everything in it will be laid bare." Yet "in keeping with his promise we are looking forward to a new heaven and a new earth, the home of righteousness" (2 Peter 3:10–13). Indeed, as Jesus promised, a day is coming when "all who are in their graves will hear his voice and come out—those who have done good will rise to live, and those who have done evil will rise to be condemned" (John 5:28–29). Or as the writer of Hebrews put it, "he will appear a second time, not to bear sin, but to bring salvation to those who are waiting for him" (Hebrews 9:28).

WILL CHRISTIANS BE IN HEAVEN DURING A SEVEN-YEAR TRIBULATION ON EARTH?

Ever since our Lord promised the early Christians that he was return-
ing to his Father's house to prepare a place for them and that he would
"come again, and receive them unto himself; that where I am, there they
may be also" (John 14:3 KJV), believers have looked forward to being
raptured or translated rather than seeing death.

—TIM LAHAYE

A prevalent theory in the church today is that, during a secret coming in the not-too-distant future, twenty-first-century followers of Jesus will be miraculously transported to heaven. During the same period, on earth, twenty-first-century Jews will experience a seven-year tribulation of mythic proportions due to the murder of the Messiah by their ancestors. In short order, two-thirds of these Jews will be reduced to bloody corpses. Coauthor of the best-selling Left Behind series Dr. Tim LaHaye uses biblical monikers such as "The Day of Israel's Calamity" to codify what he describes as "Antichrist's 'final solution' to the 'Jewish prob-lem.'"[2] According to LaHaye, "the mind-boggling terror and turmoil of the Tribulation"[3] will be a nightmarish reality far exceeding "even the Holocaust of Adolph Hitler in the twentieth century."[4] Concurrent with the carnage, a "soul harvest" will emerge due to the proselytizing prowess of 144,000 Jewish virgins. Seven years after the secret coming of Christ, there will be a second coming during which Christians will return to earth with Christ for a thousand-year semi-golden age replete with rebuilt temple and reinstituted temple sacrifices. For millions, the pretribulational rapture theory is the new norm in biblical eschatology. But is it true?

First, it is significant to note that the notion of a *secret coming of Christ* was unheard of prior to the nineteenth century. All that changed in 1831—the same year Charles Darwin left England and sailed into evolutionary infamy aboard the HMS *Beagle*. That year John Nelson Darby, a disillusioned priest, left the Church of England and joined a separatist millenarian group called the Plymouth Brethren. In general, Darby accepted the premillennial perspective of the Brethren movement. Like Darwin, however, Darby was a trendsetter. In much the same way that Darwin imposed a speculative spin on the scientific data he encountered along the coasts of Patagonia, Darby imposed a subjective spin on the scriptural data he encountered in the city of Plymouth.

Darby contended that God had two distinct people with two distinct plans and two distinct destinies. Only one of those peoples—the Jews—would suffer tribulation. The other—the church—would be removed from the world in a secret coming seven years prior to the second coming of Christ. Darby's distinctive twist on Scripture would come to be known as *dispensational eschatology*. While dispensationalism has evolved into the poster child for biblical literalism, Plymouth Brethren initially exposed to Darby's unique twist on the text considered it exegetically indefensible.

The Plymouth Brethren who resisted Darby's dispensationalism were right. The notion of a secret coming is without biblical precedent. There is not a single passage in Scripture that speaks of Christ coming secretly to resurrect and rapture Christians for seven years of heavenly bliss. Nor is there a collection of passages that can be construed to communicate a secret coming prior to the second coming of Christ. Indeed, our Lord's own words negate the notion. "A time is coming," said Jesus, "when *all* who are in their graves will hear his voice and come out—those who have done good will rise to live, and those who have done evil will rise to be condemned" (John 5:28–29; cf. Matthew 25:31–46 and Luke 12:35–48). The plain and literal sense of our Lord's words suggests a moment in the future when both the righteous and the unrighteous will be resurrected and judged together. The notion that believers will be raptured during a secret coming prior to the resurrection of unbelievers is thus an imposition on the text.

Furthermore, search as you may, you will not find in the biblical text a future seven-year Tribulation during which a vast majority of Jews will die. In fact, a future seven-year Tribulation is conspicuous by its absence in the whole of Scripture. That, of course, is not to suggest that Jews have not faced such tribulation in the past. Who can forget the terrible seven-year tribulation suffered by Jews during the beastly reign of the Old Testament antichrist—Antiochus IV Epiphanes? Onias III was prince of the covenant when the murderous Antiochus ascended the Syrian throne. He upheld the holy covenant of his God and firmly resisted the Hellenizing ways of the Greco-Syrian despot. His murder in 170 BC marked the beginning of tribulation as Antiochus purposed to destroy those who remained in covenant with their Jewish God. In 167, three years after the murder of Onias, the ultimate sacrilege befell Jerusalem. The armed forces of Antiochus rose up against the temple fortress, abolished the daily sacrifice, and set up an abomination that caused desolation.

Antiochus plundered the temple treasury, dedicated the sanctuary to the Olympian god Zeus, and sacrificed a pig on the altar. While Hellenized Jews en masse took on the mark of the Greco-Syrian beast, those who revered the God of Abraham, Isaac, and Jacob counted not their lives worthy even unto death. Against all odds they purposed to resist the Syrian juggernaut. The greatest of them was Judas Maccabaeus, who roared to victory after victory against a vastly superior Syrian superpower. In the end, he succeeded in recapturing the Temple Mount, destroying the pagan altar to the Olympian Zeus, cleansing the sanctuary, and reconsecrating the temple to Yahweh, God of Israel.

Thus, it was that on December 14, 164, seven years after Antiochus orchestrated Onias's murder and exactly three years after he had desecrated the temple fortress, abolished the daily sacrifice, and set up the abomination that causes desolation, the temple was rededicated and the daily sacrifice restored. The annual Hanukkah celebration ensures the world will ever remember the *seven-year tribulation* during the reign of the abominable Old Testament antichrist. Had God not supernaturally intervened through Judas Maccabaeus, the epicenter of Jewish spiritual and sociological identity would not just have been desecrated but destroyed.

Indeed, two centuries later the Jewish Jesus looked back on "the abomination that causes desolation spoken of by the prophet Daniel" (Matthew 24:15) to warn his followers that another seven-year tribulation was in store. In the fullness of time what Jesus declared desolate was desolated by Roman infidels. They destroyed the temple fortress and ended the daily sacrifice. This time the blood that desolated the sacred altar flowed not from the carcasses of unclean pigs but from the corpses of unbelieving Pharisees. This time the Holy of Holies was not merely desecrated by the defiling statue of a pagan god but was manifestly destroyed by the greed of despoiling soldiers. On August 30, seven years after the beginning of tribulation, the unthinkable had taken place. The very date on which the former temple had been destroyed by the Babylonian Nebuchadnezzar—the second temple was set ablaze. By September 26 all Jerusalem was in flames.

From the perspective of history, there was a three-and-a-half-year period of tribulation during the Jewish War beginning in the spring of AD 67 and ending in the fall of AD 70; however, there is no biblical precedent for doubling that time frame, driving it into the twenty-first century, and then describing it as the time of Jacob's Trouble or the time of Jewish Tribulation. Jeremiah explicitly communicates that "Jacob's Trouble" takes place during the Babylonian exile (Jeremiah 30). And Jesus emphatically places the time of "Jewish Tribulation" in the first century (Matthew 24:34). Neither can be credibly used as pretext for a Jewish holocaust in the twenty-first century. In short, there simply is no biblical warrant for a fatalistic preoccupation with a future seven-year Tribulation.

Finally, just as there is no biblical warrant for a secret coming or a future seven-year Tribulation, so too there is no biblical basis for believing in a *second chance for salvation after the second coming of Christ*. Christ is clear: all given to him by the Father will be raised up on the last day (John 6:37–40). Likewise, Paul points out that the liberation of creation goes hand in hand with the redemption of our bodies (Romans 8:18–25). Thus we can be certain that no one will be saved during a millenial semi-golden age following the second coming of Christ. The notion that our bodies are redeemed at the rapture and the earth is liberated from its bondage to decay approximately one thousand seven years later is without biblical precedent. At the second coming, the bride of Christ— the church universal—is complete. No one else can be saved.

While the notion that twenty-first-century Christians are destined for seven years of bliss and Jews are in for a holocaust of unparalleled proportions is being trumpeted in current Christianity with great bravado, it is simply not great Bible. Like Darwinian evolution, dispensational eschatology continues to morph from its humble beginnings in the British Isles. The two-people, two-plans, and two-phases dogma of Darby is now the norm, not the exception, among contemporary theologians. Dispensational doctrines are propagated through religious educational institutions and have penetrated the highest realms of influence. Those who dare question the notion of a pretribulational rapture followed by a Holy Land holocaust in which the vast majority of Jews perish are shouted down as peddlers of heresy. A pejorative phrase has even been coined for those who deny the heart of dispensational eschatology: they are dubbed "replacement theologians."

In reality nothing could be further from the truth. While dispensationalists believe Israel will *replace* the church as the focus of God's plans during the Tribulation—while two-thirds of the Jewish people will die in an unprecedented holocaust—rightly dividing the Word of Truth reveals nothing of the sort. To suggest that Jews must fulfill their national destiny as a separate entity after the rapture of Christians is an affront to Jesus in whom all the promises made to Abraham have reached their climax. The faithful remnant of Old Testament Israel and New Testament Christianity are together the one genuine seed of Abraham, and thus heirs according to the promise. This remnant is not chosen on the basis of race but rather on the basis of relationship to the resurrected Redeemer. Clothed with Christ, men, women, and children in every age and from "every tongue and tribe and nation" (Revelation 5:9) form one and only one covenant community beautifully symbolized in the book of Romans as one cultivated olive tree. Jesus is the one genuine seed of Abraham. And all clothed in Christ constitute one congruent chosen covenant community connected by the cross. "If you belong to Christ, then you are Abraham's seed, and heirs according to the promise" (Galatians 3:28–29).

In the end, there is no biblical warrant for the dispensational notion that God has two distinct people. And if God has always had only one people, the dispensational dogma collapses under the weight of Scripture. The glorious hope is not pretribulational rapture in which believers spend seven years in heaven while Jews are savaged on earth, but the promise of resurrection by which followers of the Lamb "will be with the Lord forever" (1 Thessalonians 4:17–18). In the meantime, all we need to do is be faithful.

DOES THE BIBLE TEACH A THOUSAND-YEAR SEMI-GOLDEN AGE PRIOR TO ETERNITY?

What has happened is that an idea which is based initially on only one passage in the Bible has been made the basis for prophetic schemes which are then used to interpret the whole Bible. . . . [But] the nature of the book of Revelation and the style of John's writing make it impossible to interpret the period of 1000 years literally or to suggest that it bears any relationship to historical events of the past, present or future in Palestine.

—COLIN CHAPMAN

Multitudes today hold to a theological paradigm in which followers of Christ experience life after life in the intermediate state; then life *after* life-after-life in a thousand-year semi-golden age; and finally an eternal state in which sin will be no more. As such, they suppose they will be resurrected in glorified bodies to once again experience a fallen world for a thousand years. Is this thoroughly biblical or a trendy belief?

First, we should note that though Jesus spoke repeatedly of the resurrection of the dead during his earthly sojourn, he did not so much as hint at the notion of a thousand-year semi-golden age (replete with rebuilt temple and reinstituted temple sacrifice). Instead he said, "Do not be amazed at this, for a time is coming when *all* who are in their graves will hear his voice and come out—those who have done good will rise to live, and those who have done evil will rise to be eternally condemned" (John 5:28). Moreover, when Jesus spoke with Martha concerning the resurrection of her brother he reaffirmed that Lazarus would be resurrected on the last day, not prior to a thousand-year semi-golden age (John 11:23–24).

Furthermore, nothing in Scripture suggests that those who have fallen asleep in Christ will return to a fallen earth replete with fallen earthlings. The scriptural promise that gave my father peace as he faced a terminal condition in 1997 was that one day he would return to a restored universe in which "there will be no more death or mourning or crying or pain, for the old order of things has passed away" (Revelation 21:4). Likewise, the hope respecting our preborn daughter baby Grace, who died in 2000, is that she will be resurrected to the new heavens and new earth in which there will no longer "be *any* curse" (22:3). As the apostle John makes plain, "Nothing impure will ever enter it, nor will anyone who does what is shameful or deceitful, but only those whose names are written in the Lamb's book of life" (21:27). The notion that my father and daughter, along with departed saints from time immemorial, will dwell in incorruptible immortal bodies with corruptible mortal beings for a thousand years is hardly hope. To return in the millennium with hordes of hateful humanity who number "like the sand on the seashore" and march across the breadth of the earth in opposition to the Savior and the saints (Revelation 20:8–9) is horrific. While such sensationalism sells well in post-Christian Western culture, there is simply nothing in Scripture to commend it.

Finally, while Scripture does say that "souls of those who had been beheaded because of their testimony for Jesus and because of the word of God . . . came to life and reigned with Christ a thousand years" (Revelation 20:4), nothing in the immediate or broader context leads to the conclusion that a semi-golden millennial age is in view. "Thousand" as a whole number is invariably figurative. God increased the number of the Israelites a thousand times (Deuteronomy 1:11); God keeps his covenant to a thousand generations (7:9); God owns the cattle on a thousand hills (Psalm 50:10); better is a day in God's courts than a thousand elsewhere (84:10); the least of Zion will become a thousand and the smallest a mighty nation (Isaiah 60:22); God shows love to a thousand generations (Exodus 20:6); "even if a thousand shekels were weighed out into my hands, I would not lift my hand against the king's son" (2 Samuel 18:12). And a thousand more examples (metaphorically speaking) could easily be added to the list. The point in context quite simply is this: God would allow the Beast to execute his reign of terror for "ten days"—a relatively short time—and would vindicate the beheaded, allowing them to reign with Christ for "a thousand years"—a comparatively limitless time.

In sum, the Savior did not teach the notion of a thousand-year age sandwiched between the intermediate and eternal states; by contrast, Scripture highlights the reality that the dead in Christ will return to a new heaven and earth in which the curse of sin and Satan has forever been removed; and thousand as a whole number is invariably used in figurative rather than literal fashion.

So does Scripture teach a thousand-year semi-golden age prior to the eternal state? Absolutely not! When eschatological models are imposed on the text, the tapestry is undone and the loose ends dangle ignominiously. When scriptural synergy takes precedence, the majesty of Scripture culminates in "the new Jerusalem, coming down out of heaven from God, prepared as a bride beautifully dressed for her husband" (Revelation 21:2).

CHAPTER
TWELVE

⋮

How does the afterlife affect my life now?

WHEN DOES ETERNAL LIFE BEGIN?

Eternal life does not begin with death; it begins with faith.

—Samuel Shoemaker

While many suppose that eternal life begins the moment we die, the reality is that our eternal life begins the moment we embrace the Savior who died in our place and stretches on throughout eternity. Therefore, eternal life exists in all three phases of life: it is a current commodity in this life; it continues as ongoing reality in the life after life; and it is consummated as ultimate reality in the life *after* life-after-life.

First, just as physical birth can never be undone, so too spiritual birth can never be undone. Thus, those who are in Christ experience eternal life as a present possession. Our Master provides ultimate assurance for this reality: "I tell you the truth, whoever hears my word and believes him who sent me *has* eternal life and will not be condemned; he has crossed over from death to life" (John 5:24). As those who "participate in the divine nature" (2 Peter 1:4), we taste in time "the powers of the coming age" (Hebrews 6:5)—what Watchman Nee aptly referred to as "the normal Christian life."[1] We experience eternal life as through a glass darkly—yet even now we experience it in this life!

Furthermore, we may rightly say that our experience of eternal life will be significantly enhanced in the intermediate state (life after life). As the apostle Paul sums up: "To depart" the body is to "be with Christ" (Philippians 1:23). Put another way, with the death of the body we experience a new realm of soul satisfaction. This satisfaction is of such surpassing significance that "to live is Christ" but "to die is gain." Thus, says Paul, "I am torn between the two: I desire to depart and be with Christ, which is better by far; but it is more necessary for you that I remain in the body" (Philippians 1:21, 23–24). While the full experience of eternal life in the intermediate state requires speculation for those yet in the body, of one thing we can be certain. It will be, as Paul exudes, "better by far."

Finally, our eternal life will be consummated in the eternal state (life *after* life-after-life). When Christ returns with a loud command, with the voice of the archangel, and with the trumpet call of God, we will be gloriously transformed in resurrection. In the intermediate state our soul is "absent from the body" and "present with the Lord" (2 Corinthians 5:8). But in the eternal state our souls will return to resurrected bodies; we will experience a restored universe; and we will forever commune with a resurrected Christ as we learn and grow and develop without error.

In the present we experience eternal life as through a veil; in the life after life that veil will be removed and eternal life will continue in the presence of the King; and in the life *after* life-after-life we will experience eternal life as the New Jerusalem coming down out of heaven from God. On that day the prayer, "Thy kingdom come, Thy will be done in earth, as it is in heaven" (Matthew 6:10 KJV) will find final resolution in resurrection glory.

WHAT MUST I DO TO INHERIT ETERNAL LIFE?

Give up yourself, and you will find your real self. Lose your life and you will save it. Submit to death, death of your ambitions and favorite wishes every day and death of your whole body in the end: submit with every fiber of your being, and you will find eternal life. Keep back nothing. Nothing that you have not given away will ever be really yours. Nothing in you that has not died will ever be raised from the dead. Look for yourself, and you will find in the long run only hatred, loneliness, despair, rage, ruin, and decay. But look for Christ and you will find Him, and with Him everything else thrown in.

—C. S. LEWIS

A rich young ruler of rank and reputation asked Jesus Christ this very question. Not just *a* question—*the* question! "What must I do to inherit eternal life?" (Matthew 19:16–30; Mark 10:17–30; Luke 18:18–30). Christ's answer was shocking: "If you want to be perfect, go sell your possessions and give to the poor, and you will have treasure in heaven. Then come follow me." This was not the first time that Christ had set the bar impossibly high. In the Sermon on the Mount he had gone so far as to tell his hearers, "Be perfect, therefore, as your heavenly Father is perfect" (Matthew 5:48). The disciples were "amazed, and said to each other, 'Who then can be saved?'" (Matthew 19:25 KJV). If that is the standard, how can anyone inherit eternal life? Thankfully there is a resolution to the conundrum. It is encapsulated in three words: *realize, repent,* and *receive.*

First, you and I must *realize* we are sinners. Apart from the realization that we are sinners in need of a Savior we have no hope of salvation. In the aforementioned conversation with the rich young ruler Jesus said to him, "If you want to enter life, obey the commandments" (Matthew 19:17). The young man's response was the very embodiment of self-righteousness: "All these I have kept since I was a boy" (Mark 10:20). A lesser teacher might have laughed out loud. Jesus did not. Instead he opened the floodgates of understanding. "If you want to be perfect, go sell your possessions and give to the poor, and you will have treasure in heaven. Then come follow me" (Matthew 19:21 NKJV).

In saying this, Jesus exposed the utter folly of supposing that anyone can be good enough to be acceptable to God based on his or her own merit. Sin is not only doing that which we should not do; it is failing to do that which we should. Put another way, just as there are sins of *commission* (sins we commit), so too there are sins of *omission* (the sin of omitting to do all we should). Who among us can say we have selflessly or steadfastly cared for those who are in need? The words of the Master struck their target like a heat-seeking missile. The rich young ruler did not protest or argue. Instead, as noted in the gospel of Mark, his "face fell" (Mark 10:22). And "he went away sad, because he had great wealth" (Matthew 19:22).

Furthermore, when we realize we are sinners in need of a Savior, we must also be willing to *repent. Repentance* is an old English word that describes a willingness to turn from self-sufficiency to embrace the all-sufficiency of the Savior. It quite literally means a U-turn on the road of life—a change of heart and a change of mind. To turn from self-sufficiency is to recognize that Christ and Christ alone can attain to the credential of sinlessness. Moses could not do that, nor could Isaiah. When the most righteous man in Israel caught a glimpse of the holiness of God, he cried out in recognition of his own sinfulness, "Woe to me! . . . I am ruined! For I am a man of unclean lips, and I live among a people of unclean lips, and my eyes have seen the King, the LORD Almighty" (Isaiah 6:5).

The Pharisees, too, fell far short. They tithed their mint and cumin but neglected the weightier matters of the Law (Matthew 23:23). Even Paul, who wrote two-thirds of the New Testament epistles, recognized how far he lived from sinlessness. "What I do is not the good I want to do," he confessed to the Roman believers. "No, the evil I do not want to do—this I keep on doing" (Romans 7:19). The rich young ruler may well have been upright by worldly standards. But he was hardly sinless. Thus, in saying, *"If you want to be perfect*, go, sell your possessions and give to the poor, and you will have treasure in heaven," Jesus was not reproving the young man's wealth. From Joseph and Abraham to Joseph of Arimathea, Scripture is replete with wealthy believers. Instead, he was revealing the young man's wickedness. He loved goods far more than he loved God. Thus, like all others, he stood in need of repentance.

Finally, the realization of sin and a willingness to repent must inevitably lead to a readiness to *receive*. To truly receive is to trust in and depend on Jesus Christ alone to be the Lord of our lives here and now and our Savior for all eternity. And this the rich young ruler was not willing to do. When Jesus invited the young ruler to follow him, the young man turned and went away. Christ's words had no doubt produced within him recognition of sin. But it takes more than *knowledge*. He likely agreed that Christ and Christ alone could attain to the credential of sinlessness. But it takes more than *agreement*. To *receive* means to be willing to follow Jesus and trust in him alone for eternal life.

When you are sick you can know that a particular medicine can cure you. You can agree that the medicine has cured thousands before you. But until you trust the medicine enough to take it, it cannot cure you. In like manner, you can know about Jesus Christ. You can agree that he has saved others, but until you place your trust in him and enter into the family of faith, you remain unsaved. The requirements for eternal life are not based on what you can do in keeping the commandments as the rich young ruler professed to do. Rather, eternal life is solely dependent on what Christ has done in your stead. Put another way, the gospel is not *do*—it is *done* through the person and work of Jesus Christ. We cannot work *for* our salvation; we can only in gratitude work *from* our salvation. And as with the rich young ruler, Christ stands ever ready to exchange his perfection for our imperfection.

In sum then, according to Jesus, those who *realize* they are sinners, *repent* of their sins, and *receive* him as Savior and Lord are "born again" (John 3:3)—not physically but spiritually. The reality of our salvation does not depend on our feelings but rather on the promise of the Savior, who said, "I tell you the truth, whoever hears my word and believes him who sent me has eternal life and will not be condemned; he has crossed over from death to life" (John 5:24). The choice therefore is to turn and follow Jesus, or like the rich young ruler, to turn in the other direction.

HOW CAN THOSE WHO INHERIT ETERNAL LIFE GROW IN SPIRITUAL STRENGTH?

The greatest issue facing the world today, with all its heartbreaking needs, is whether those who, by profession or culture, are identified

as "Christians" will become disciples—students, apprentices, practi-
tioners—of Jesus Christ, steadily learning from him how to live the life
of the Kingdom of the Heavens into every corner of human existence.

—DALLAS WILLARD

According to the Beloved Disciple, those who realize that they are sinners, repent of their sin, and receive him as Savior and Lord may know
of a surety that they *have* eternal life. Not *might have* or *could have*—
but *have* eternal life. Thus, says John, "I write these things to you who
believe in the name of the Son of God so that *you may know that you
have eternal life*" (1 John 5:13). But with this life must come growth. It
is crucial, therefore, to know the *ABC*s of spiritual growth (*Amen, Bible,
Church*) so we may grow in spiritual strength and vigor.

First and foremost, we must develop intimacy with the One who
has designated himself "the *Amen*, the faithful and true witness, the
ruler of God's creation" (Revelation 3:14). You are likely familiar with
the word "amen," but have you ever taken time to consider what it
really entails? Not only is it a title by which Jesus identifies himself, but
it means "may it be so in accordance with the will of God." As such, it
is recognition of the sovereignty of God. In effect, it is a way of saying,
"Thank God this world is under his control, not mine!" Moreover, it is
daily recognition that our wills must be submitted to God's will. In the
yielded life there is great peace in knowing that the One who taught us
to pray "your will be done" has every detail of our lives under control.
He will not spare us from trial and tribulation but will rather use the
fiery furnace to purge impurities from our lives. In this world we will
have trouble, but as the Master so eloquently put it, "Take heart! I have
overcome the world" (John 16:33).

The "amen" at the end of every one of our prayers reminds us to live
with eternity in mind. It is a constant reminder to stop seeing prayer as
merely a method by which to obtain things from God and to start seeing
prayer as an opportunity to build intimacy with the One with whom we

will fellowship for all eternity. Put another way, prayer is a foretaste of something we will experience forever. Paradise lost will one day become paradise restored and a whole lot more. For we will experience something not even Adam and Eve experienced—face-to-face communication with the very One who modeled the principles of prayer and who bequeathed to his disciples the model prayer (Matthew 6:9–14).

Furthermore, to grow in spiritual strength it is crucial that we spend time reading God's written revelation—the *Bible*. The Bible not only forms the foundation of an effective prayer life but also is foundational to every other aspect of daily living. While prayer is our primary way of communicating with God, the Bible is God's primary way of communicating with us. Thus, nothing should take precedence over getting into the Word and getting the Word into us. If we fail to eat well-balanced meals on a regular basis, we will eventually suffer the physical consequences. What is true of the outer man is likewise true of the inner man. If we do not regularly feed on the Word of God, we will starve spiritually. As Jesus armed himself with "the sword of the Spirit, which is the word of God" (Ephesians 6:17), so must we. Armed with the puny sword of reason, we stand impotent before an arch-fiend who has studied us thoroughly and is intimately acquainted with all of our vulnerabilities. Armed with the sword of the Spirit, however, we are a terror to Satan and can stand strong in the face of his fiercest temptations.

Wielding the sword of the Spirit, which is the Word of God, involves *mining* the Bible for all its wealth, *memorizing* the Bible for all its worth, and *meditating* upon its words. God has called us to write his Word on the tablets of our hearts (Proverbs 7:1–3; cf. Deuteronomy 6:6), and with the call he has provided the ability commensurate with the task (2 Corinthians 9:8; Philippians 4:13). The Bible in essence is sixty-six love letters from God, addressed specifically to us. Thus, it stands to reason that we would continually meditate upon them. Our communication with God is only as inspired as our intake of Scripture. Indeed, meditation is a crucial connection between the ingestion of Scripture and an effective prayer life. In the ultimate spiritual battle, Jesus took up the sword of the Spirit, which is the Word of God. He had mined, memorized, and meditated on Scripture. Thus, when the slanderer sought to tempt the Savior to turn stones into bread, Jesus was prepared. "It is written," he said, "Man does not live on bread alone, but on every word that comes from the mouth of God" (Matthew 4:4).

Finally, those who have inherited eternal life as a present possession will gain spiritual strength and vibrancy by being active participants in a healthy, well-balanced *church*. In Scripture, the church is referred to as the body of Christ. Just as our body is one and yet has many parts, so too the body of Christ is one but is composed of many members. Those who receive Christ as the Savior and Lord of their lives are already part of the church universal. It is crucial, however, that all Christians become vital, reproducing members of a local body of believers as well.

The first sign of a healthy, well-balanced church is commitment to the worship of God through prayer, praise, and proclamation. Prayer is so inextricably woven into the fabric of worship that it would be unthinkable to experience gathering together on the Lord's Day without it. Praise, likewise, is axiomatic to worship. Scripture urges us to "speak to one another with psalms, hymns and spiritual songs" (Ephesians 5:19). Along with prayer and praise, proclamation is critical to experiencing vibrant worship. For it is through the proclamation of God's Word that believers are edified, exhorted, encouraged, and equipped.

A healthy, well-balanced church is also evidenced through its oneness. Christ breaks the barriers of gender, race, and social standing and unites us as one under the banner of his love. Oneness in Christ is tangibly manifested through community, confession, and contribution. Community is manifested through baptism, which symbolizes our entrance into a body of believers who are one in Christ. In like fashion, the Lord's Table is an expression of oneness. As we all partake of the same elements, we partake of Christ, through whom we are one. A further expression of oneness is our common confession of faith—a core set of beliefs, which have been rightly referred to as "essential Christianity." As with community and confession, we experience oneness through the contribution of our time, talent, and treasure. The apostle Paul exhorts us to "share with God's people who are in need. Practice hospitality" (Romans 12:13).

Lastly, in addition to worship and oneness, a healthy, well-balanced church is one committed to equipping believers to be effective witnesses to *what* they believe, *why* they believe, and *Who* they believe. The *what* of our faith is the good news of the gospel. The gospel of Christ should become such a part of our vocabulary that presenting it becomes second nature. We also must be equipped to share *why* we believe what we believe. As Peter put it, "always be prepared to give an answer to everyone who asks you to give the reason for the hope that you have. But do this with gentleness and respect" (1 Peter 3:15). And then we must be empowered to communicate the *Who* of our faith. Virtually every theological heresy begins with a misconception of the nature of God. We know we have discovered a healthy, well-balanced body of believers when God is worshipped in Spirit and in truth through prayer, praise, and proclamation; where oneness is tangibly manifested through community, confession, and contribution; and where believers are being equipped to communicate what they believe, why they believe, and Who they believe.

In sum, the *ABCs* of spiritual growth (*Amen, Bible, Church*) are an enduring reminder to inheritors of eternal life that with spiritual birth must come spiritual growth and spiritual vibrancy. As together we partake of the Lord's Table we are forevermore reminded that Jesus is "the bread of life" (John 6:35). He is the aftertaste of our deliverance and the foretaste of a coming kingdom in which "the dwelling of God is with men, and he will live with them. They will be his people, and God himself will be with them and be their God" (Revelation 21:3).

WHAT IS THE CONNECTION BETWEEN SUNDAYS, THE SACRAMENTS, AND OUR AFTERLIFE?

Within the sacramental world, past and present are one. Together they point forward to the still-future liberation.

—N. T. WRIGHT

The disciples were radically transformed by the resurrection. Peter, once afraid of being exposed as a follower of Christ by a young woman, was transformed into a lion of the faith as a result of encountering the resurrected Christ. Paul, a ceaseless persecutor of early Christians, encountered the risen Christ and became the chief evangelist to the Gentiles. And an entire community of Jews willingly transformed the spiritual and sociological traditions underscoring their national identity —including Sabbath and the sacraments.

First, they transitioned the Sabbath to Sunday. Within weeks of Christ's resurrection, thousands of Jews willingly changed a longstanding theological tradition that had given them their national identity. God himself provided the early church with a new pattern of worship through Christ's resurrection on the first day of the week, his subsequent Sunday appearances, and the Spirit's Sunday descent (Matthew 28:1–10; John 20:26; Acts 2:1; 20:7; 1 Corinthians 16:2).

For the emerging Christian church, the most dangerous snare was a failure to recognize that Jesus was the substance that fulfilled the symbol of the Sabbath. "Therefore," says Paul, "do not let anyone judge you by what you eat or drink, or with regard to a religious festival, a New Moon celebration or a Sabbath day. These are a shadow of the things that were to come; the reality, however, is found in Christ" (Colossians 2:16–17). Paul's list here is instructive. Those who became Jews— whether Rahab, Ruth, or "people of other nationalities" (Esther 8:17)— were brought into a system of shadows that pointed forward to the coming of the Messiah. With the coming of Christ, such Old Covenant lists (e.g., Ezekiel 45:17; Hosea 2:11) were no longer the point. They served as shadows (Colossians 2:17). The day of worship was now a celebration of the "rest" we have through Christ, who delivers us from sin and the grave (Hebrews 4:1–11). The day of resurrection had become the day of worship.

Through his resurrection Jesus demonstrated that he does not stand in a line of peers with Abraham, Buddha, or Confucius. He is the Creator—they are his creations. Easter is the celebration that Christ, not Caesar, is Lord. Through his resurrection the veil between heaven and earth has been parted and one day will disappear. The resurrection power that once flooded the corpse of Christ will flood the cosmos in the renewal of all things. Lest we ever forget, each Sunday living stones in the temple of God gather together in celebration of Christianity's seminal event—the resurrection of Christ and vicariously that of Christians.

Furthermore, as with the setting apart of the first day of the week, the setting apart of the saved through the first act of obedience is inextricably linked to the reality of resurrection. Prior to Christ's resurrection, Gentile converts to Judaism were baptized in the name of the God of Israel. After resurrection, converts to Christianity were baptized in the name of Jesus (Acts 2:36–41). In doing so, Christians equated Jesus with Israel's God.

In his epistle to the Romans, Paul elevates the sacrament of baptism by equating it to death and resurrection. The first act of obedience was dying to the world in which Caesar was lord and rising to newness of life in a kingdom in which Christ is Lord. "We were therefore buried with him through baptism into death in order that, just as Christ was raised from the dead through the glory of the Father, we too may live a new life. If we have been united with him like this in his death, we will certainly also be united with him in his resurrection" (Romans 6:4–5). Likewise, in his epistle to the Colossian Christians, Paul speaks of being buried with Christ in baptism and raised with Christ in newness of life (Colossians 2:12).

While baptism is often relegated to little more than a water sport in contemporary Christianity, it was a matter of life and death for believers living in the epicenter of a Caesar cult. Through baptism they were overtly denying the lordship of Caesar. Thus, more often than not, being baptized was tantamount to signing a death warrant. In place of hair gel and dry clothing, the newly baptized might well be dressed in tar jackets and set ablaze. The world was not worthy of them. They had glimpsed a new heaven and a new earth beyond the veil. They knew that in resurrection the kingdom of God had broken in and would one day fill heaven and earth.

Finally, the elements of the Lord's Table find ultimate fulfillment in the resurrection of all things. As such, Easter and the Eucharist are inextricably woven as one. In place of the Passover meal, those who believe that Jesus Christ is Lord of all celebrate Communion. Imagine the irony. Jesus was slaughtered in grotesque and humiliating fashion, yet his disciples remembered his broken body and shed blood with joy. Only resurrection can account for that!

Each year the Jews celebrated Passover in remembrance of God's sparing the firstborn sons in the homes of the Israelite families that were marked by the blood of the Passover lamb (Luke 22; cf. Exodus 11–12). Jesus' celebration of the Passover meal with his disciples on the night of his arrest symbolically points to the fact that he is the ultimate Passover Lamb "who takes away the sin of the world" (John 1:29). Though the Last Supper and the corresponding sacrament of Communion serve as the antitype of the Passover meal, they also point forward to ultimate fulfillment in "the wedding supper of the Lamb" (Revelation 19:9; cf. Luke 22:15–18). On that glorious day the purified bride—true Israel—will be united with her Bridegroom in the new heaven and the new earth (Revelation 21:1–2). Salvation has come. It eagerly awaits consummation.

We partake of the elements of Communion "in remembrance" both rearward and forward (Luke 22:19). Rearward, in remembrance of Jesus' broken body and shed blood for the complete remission of sins. Forward, as a pointer toward the new heaven and a new earth in which resurrected Christians will forever commune with a resurrected Christ. His resurrection is a foretaste of an eternal banquet table. His resurrection is the inauguration of a heaven and earth as one. A resurrected reality in which death no longer is part of the equation. "Blessed are those who are invited to the wedding supper of the Lamb!" (Revelation 19:9).

Of one thing I am certain—if twenty-first-century Christians would grasp the significance of resurrection like first-century Christians did, their lives would be inexorably transformed. Each Sunday is a celebration of resurrection; each baptism is fresh evidence that we are raised with him in newness of life. Evidence of taking up the cross, of living the crucified life, of awaiting the reappearance of Christ and the kingdom— each time we partake of the elements we remember him in whom all things find ultimate resolution in resurrection.

ACKNOWLEDGMENTS

First, I would like to express my deepest appreciation for Byron Williamson and the team at Worthy Publishing for urging and inspiring me to make *AfterLife* my next writing project. With the recent spate of books on near-death experiences, the timing could not have been better. Byron in particular has been a valued friend and counselor throughout the entirety of my writing career. My prayer is that God would be pleased to use this volume to bring clarity of purpose to the present life, a laser-sharp perspective on life after life, and passion and perseverance for the life *after* life-after-life we will experience forever.

Furthermore, I am, as always, indebted to my friend and colaborer Stephen Ross, who painstakingly attends to every jot and tittle. Now in our third decade of working together, we continue to find joy in the journey. Likewise, I am privileged once again to work with Jennifer Stair as my editor. Her enthusiasm for the project is matched only by the excellence of her work.

Finally, I am grateful for a solid base on the homefront as well as on the workfront. I am particularly appreciative of my colaborers at the Christian Research Institute, many of whom have been with me for well over two decades. Most of all, I am grateful that God would condescend to use me in even the smallest of ways.

NOTES

SOMEDAY YOU WILL DIE—THEN WHAT?

1. Raymond Moody Jr., *Life after Life* (Covington, GA: Mockingbird, 1975).

2. Betty J. Eadie with Curtis Taylor, *Embraced by the Light* (Placerville, CA: Gold Leaf Press, 1992).

3. Don Piper with Cecil Murphey, *90 Minutes in Heaven: A True Story of Death and Life* (Grand Rapids: Revell, 2004), 129.

4. Ibid., 34–35.

5. Ibid., 24.

6. Ibid., 27.

7. Ibid., 22.

8. "Don Piper tells his experience of Going to Heaven and Coming Back!!" *700 Club*, CBN, http://www.youtube.com/watch?v=wx6FBUD_Amc (approximately 8:35 mark).

9. Bill Wiese, "23 Minutes in Hell—Bill Wiese Hell Testimony (Extended Hell Version)," http://www.youtube.com/watch?v=nmrTfyM-hbY (see at approximately 23 minutes, accessed December 7, 2012). Though Wiese says his senses were very keen during his twenty-three-minute experience so that he precisely knew such details as the 300-degree temperature and four-thousand-mile distance from the surface to hell's location at the center of the earth, his story evolves, for on other occasions he says he does not know what the temperature was (see "23 Minutes in Hell - Bill Wiese [Newest Version - Dec 2006] More Details," http://www.youtube.com/watch?v=ysqXNRdZ4V8 [see at approximately 2.5 minutes, accessed December 7, 2012]).

10. See "Special Guests Todd and Colton Burpo—Part 2," http://www.youtube.com/watch?v=4pgMOS8Q8nk&feature=related, viewed March 22, 2012.

11. Ibid.

12. Todd Burpo with Lynn Vincent, *Heaven Is for Real: A Little Boy's Astounding Story of His Trip to Heaven and Back* (Nashville: Thomas Nelson, 2010), 136. Concerning the theological question of whether or not infants go to heaven when they die, for example, Burpo writes, "We had wanted to believe that our unborn child had gone to heaven. Even though the Bible is largely silent on this point, we had accepted it by faith. But now, we had an eyewitness [in Colton]: a daughter we had never met was waiting eagerly for us in eternity" (97). Colton seems also to have settled for Burpo the right interpretation of Revelation 9:6–10— the images presented in this passage are not mere symbols for kingdoms or military machinery; rather, they are actual monsters whom Burpo himself will fight with either sword or bow and arrow (Colton can't recall which) in the battle of Armageddon (135–39).

13. Eben Alexander, MD, *Proof of Heaven: A Neurosurgeon's Journey into the Afterlife* (New York: Simon and Schuster, 2012), 9, 41, 71, 78, 135, 148, emphasis in original.

14. Ibid., 163.

15. Ibid., 47, 48, 76, 156.

16. Ibid., 164.

17. Mary K. Baxter, *A Divine Revelation of Hell* (Springdale, PA: Whitaker House, 1993).

18. Kevin and Alex Malarkey, *The Boy Who Came Back from Heaven: A Remarkable Account of Miracles, Angels, and Life beyond This World* (Carol Stream, IL: Tyndale, 2011), front cover, x.

19. Ibid., 30.

20. Ibid., 48.

21. Alexander, *Proof of Heaven*, 109, 163.

22. Mark Hitchcock, *55 Answers to Questions about Life after Death* (Sisters, OR: Multnomah, 2005), 134–35.

PART 1—LIFE *AFTER* LIFE-AFTER-LIFE: THE ETERNAL HEAVEN AND EARTH

CHAPTER 1. WHAT IS HEAVEN ABOUT?

1. See NIV and ESV footnotes at Revelation 21:16; cf. NASB and ESV notes. Some calculate "12,000 stadia" to be about fourteen hundred miles; others think it is about fifteen hundred miles.

CHAPTER 2. WHAT HAPPENS TO US IN HEAVEN?

1. A. A. Hodge, *Evangelical Theology*, quoted in Peter Toon, *Heaven and Hell* (Nashville: Thomas Nelson, 1986), 158.
2. N. T. Wright, *Hebrews for Everyone* (Louisville, KY: Westminster John Knox Press, 2004), 121.
3. Gilbert K. Chesterton, *Orthodoxy* (New York: John Lane,1909), 103.

CHAPTER 3. WHAT IS HEAVEN LIKE?

1. Peter Kreeft, *Everything You Ever Wanted to Know about Heaven, but Never Dreamed of Asking* (San Francisco: Ignatius Press,1990), 45. Kreeft cites Thomas Aquinas on this point.
2. Billy Graham, *Nearing Home: Life, Faith, and Finishing Well* (Nashville: Thomas Nelson, 2011), 93.

CHAPTER 4. WHAT'S UP WITH HELL?

1. Bill Wiese, "23 Minutes in Hell—Bill Wiese Hell Testimony (Extended Hell Version)," http://www.youtube.com/watch?v=nmrTfyM-hbY (see at approximately 23 minutes, accessed December 7, 2012). Though Wiese says his senses were

very keen during his twenty-three-minute experience so that he precisely knew such details as the 300-degree temperature and four-thousand-mile distance from the surface to hell's location at the center of the earth, his story evolves, for on other occasions he says he does not know what the temperature was (see "23 Minutes in Hell - Bill Wiese (Newest Version - Dec 2006) More Details," http://www.youtube.com/watch?v=ysqXNRdZ4V8 [see at approximately 2.5 minutes, accessed December 7, 2012]).

2. See N. T. Wright, *Surprised by Hope: Rethinking Heaven, the Resurrection, and the Mission of the Church* (New York: HarperOne, 2008), 175–83.

3. See Hank Hanegraaff, "Frauds, Fictions, Fabrications, and Fantasies," *Christian Research Journal* 18, no. 3 (1996): 54–55; and Rich Buhler, "Background on the Drilling to Hell Story," at http://www.truthorfiction.com/rumors/d/drilltohellfacts.htm, accessed August 14, 2012.

4. Clark Pinnock, "The Conditional View," in William Crockett, ed., *Four Views on Hell* (Grand Rapids: Zondervan, 1992).

5. David L. Edwards and John Stott, *Essentials* (London: Hodder & Stoughton, 1988), 313–20.

6. Everett Rosenfeld, "Fond Farewells: John Stott, Theologian, 90," *Time*, August 15, 2011, http://www.time.com/time/specials/packages/article/0,28804,2101745_2102136_2102268,00.htm, accessed August 11, 2012.

7. Clark H. Pinnock, "The Destruction of the Finally Impenitent," *Criswell Theological Review* 4, no. 2 (1990): 243–59.

8. Millard Erickson, *The Evangelical Mind and Heart* (Grand Rapids: Baker, 1993), 152.

9. Edwards and Stott, *Essentials*, 320.

10. R. C. H. Lenski, *Commentary on the New Testament: The Interpretation of St. Luke's Gospel* (Peabody, MA: Hendrickson, 2001; originally published 1946 by Wartburg Press), 849–50.

11. Charles Haddon Spurgeon, "The Resurrection of the Dead," sermon preached February 17, 1856, online at http://www. spurgeon.org/sermons/0066.htm, accessed August 14, 2012.

12. Lenski, *Commentary on the New Testament*, 854–55.

13. Charles Haddon Spurgeon, *Sermons of the Rev. C. H. Spurgeon*, 2nd series (New York: Sheldon and Company, 1859), 275.

14. Widely attributed to G. K. Chesterton; if not an actual statement by him, it is certainly consonant with his thinking.

15. Norman L. Geisler, *Baker Encyclopedia of Christian Apologetics* (Grand Rapids: Baker, 1999), 313.

16. This quote is widely attributed to Reagan, but I have not been able to track down a specific source. If he didn't say it as quoted, the condemnation of socialism is nonetheless quite consistent with his expressed views.

17. J. P. Moreland, quoted in Gary R. Habermas and J. P. Moreland, *Beyond Death: Exploring the Evidence for Immortality* (Wheaton, IL: Crossway Books, 1998), 296.

18. Edwards and Stott, *Essentials*, 313–20.

PART 2—LIFE AFTER LIFE:
THE TRANSITIONAL HEAVEN

1. Hillel Italie, Associated Press, "Literati Gore Vidal Was a Celebrated Author, Playwright," *Charlotte Observer*, August 2, 2012.

2. Ibid.

3. Gore Vidal, "Armageddon?" in *United States*: Essays 1952-1992 (New York: Random House, 1993; Broadway Books, 2001), 1006.Citations refer to the Broadway edition.

4. These arguments are drawn from Gary R. Habermas and J. P. Moreland, *Beyond Death: Exploring the Evidence for Immortality* (Wheaton, IL: Crossway, 1998).

5. N. T. Wright, *Surprised by Hope: Rethinking Heaven, the Resurrection, and the Mission of the Church* (New York: HarperOne, 2008), 115.

6. Carl Sagan, *Cosmos* (New York: Random House, 1980), 1.

7. Vidal, "Armageddon?" in *United States*, 1006.

CHAPTER 5. WHAT HAPPENS TO US BETWEEN DEATH AND HEAVEN?

1. The arguments for the existence of a substantive human soul on the basis of libertarian freedom, legality, and logic are drawn from philosopher J. P. Moreland in Gary R. Habermas and J. P. Moreland, *Beyond Death: Exploring the Evidence for Immortality* (Wheaton, IL: Crossway Books, 1998).

2. This is a very rough generalization, as different tissues and cell types regenerate at different rates. "Every one of us completely regenerates our own skin every 7 days. . . . Every single cell in our skeleton is replaced every 7 years" (http://stemcell.stanford.edu/research/). The exception appears to be our nervous system, though questions about regeneration of these cells remain.

3. Hank Hanegraaff, *Resurrection* (Nashville: W Publishing, 2000).

4. Randy Alcorn, *Heaven* (Wheaton, IL: Tyndale, 2004), 58.

5. Ibid.

6. *Seventh-Day Adventists Believe . . . A Biblical Exposition of Fundamental Doctrines*, 2nd ed. (Silver Spring, MD: Ministerial Association of the General Conference of Seventh-Day Adventists, 2005), 94–95, 390–91.

CHAPTER 6. WHAT IS THE TRANSITIONAL HEAVEN LIKE?

1. Billy Graham, *The Heaven Answer Book* (Nashville: Thomas Nelson, 2012), 124.
2. N. T. Wright, *Surprised by Hope: Rethinking Heaven, the Resurrection, and the Mission of the Church* (New York: HarperOne, 2008), 111.
3. Ibid., 115.

CHAPTER 7. ARE NEAR-DEATH EXPERIENCES THE REAL THING?

1. Raymond Moody Jr., *Life after Life* (Covington, GA: Mockingbird, 1975).
2. Betty J. Eadie with Curtis Taylor, *Embraced by the Light* (Placerville, CA: Gold Leaf Press, 1992).
3. Elizabeth L. Hillstrom, *Testing the Spirits* (Downers Grove, IL: InterVarsity Press, 1995), 82.
4. Mary Neal, quoted in Mark Galli, "Incredible Journeys," *Christianity Today* 56, no. 11 (2012): 25.
5. Todd Burpo with Lynn Vincent, *Heaven Is for Real: A Little Boy's Astounding Story of His Trip to Heaven and Back* (Nashville: Thomas Nelson, 2010), 87.
6. Hillstrom, *Testing the Spirits*, 83.
7. Maurice Rawlings, *Beyond Death's Door* (Nashville: Thomas Nelson, 1978).
8. C. A. Garfield, *Between Life and Death*, ed. Robert Kastenbaum (New York: Spring, 1979), 54–55, in Robert Kastenbaum, *Is There Life After Death?* (New York, Prentice Hall, 1984), 18.
9. Michael Sabom, "The Shadow of Death," part 1, *Christian Research Journal* 26, no. 2 (2003), online at http://www.equip.org/PDF/DD282-1.pdf, accessed August 15, 2012.

10. Burpo with Vincent, *Heaven Is for Real*, 97.

11. Ibid., 95.

12. Ibid., 136.

13. R. C. Sproul, *The Last Days According to Jesus* (Grand Rapids: Baker, 1998).

14. Burpo with Vincent, *Heaven Is for Real*, 135ff.

15. Hal Lindsey, *Apocalypse Code* (Palos Verdes, CA: Western Front, 1997), back cover.

16. Ibid., 37, 41.

17. Ibid., 41.

18. Ibid., 42.

19. Burpo with Vincent, *Heaven Is for Real*, 138.

20. Ibid., 137.

21. R. C. Sproul, *Knowing Scripture* (Downers Grove, IL: InterVarsity, 1977), 46.

22. Don Piper with Cecil Murphey, *90 Minutes in Heaven: A True Story of Death and Life* (Grand Rapids: Revell, 2004), 13.

23. "700 Club: 90 Minutes in Heaven," CBN TV, http://www.cbn.com/media/player/index.aspx?s=/vod/SUB90_DonPiper_022411_WS (approximately 8:15 mark); also here: "Don Piper tells his experience of Going to Heaven and Coming Back!!" http://www.youtube.com/watch?v=wx6FBUD_Amc (both links accessed November 15, 2012).

24. Piper with Murphey, *90 Minutes in Heaven*, 129.

25. See "Special Guests Todd and Colton Burpo – Part 2," *Today with Marilyn and Sarah*, http://www.youtube.com/watch?v=4pgMOS8Q8nk&feature=related, accessed March 22, 2012.

26. Kevin and Alex Malarkey, *The Boy Who Came Back from Heaven: A Remarkable Account of Miracles, Angels, and Life Beyond this World* (Carol Stream, IL: Tyndale, 2011), 48.

27. Burpo with Vincent, *Heaven Is for Real*, 144.

28. Akiane and Foreli Kramarik, *Akiane: Her Life, Her Art, Her Poetry* (Nashville: Thomas Nelson, 2006), 27.

29. Betty J. Eadie with Curtis Taylor, *Embraced by the Light* (Placerville, CA: Gold Leaf Press, 1992), 42.

30. Mormon Apostle Bruce McConkie writes, "Christ was begotten by an Immortal Father in the same way that mortal men are begotten by mortal fathers" (Bruce R. McConkie, *Mormon Doctrine*, 2nd ed. [Salt Lake City: Bookcraft, 1966], 547). Long before McConkie, Mormon Apostle Orson Pratt explained that "the fleshly body of Jesus required a Mother as well as a Father. Therefore, the Father and Mother of Jesus, according to the flesh, must have been associated together in the capacity of Husband and Wife: hence the Virgin Mary must have been, for the time being, the lawful wife of God the Father" (Orson Pratt, *The Seer* [Washington, DC, 1853–54], 158–59, quoted in Ron Rhodes and Marian Bodine, *Reasoning from the Scriptures with the Mormons* [Eugene, OR: Harvest House, 1995], 268–69). Brigham Young extrapolated that Mary must have had at least two husbands. Said Young, "The man Joseph, the husband of Mary, did not, that we know of, have more than one wife, but *Mary the wife of Joseph had another husband*—that is, God the Father" (Brigham Young, *Deseret News*, October 10, 1866, quoted in Jerald and Sandra Tanner, *The Changing World of Mormonism* [Chicago: Moody Press, 1980], 180, emphasis in Tanner).

31. Joseph Smith, *History of the Church of Jesus Christ of Latter-day Saints* (Salt Lake City: Deseret Book, 1978), 6:305.

32. Lorenzo Snow [Fifth Mormon President], *The Millennial Star*, 54:404 (1840).

33. Eben Alexander, MD, *Proof of Heaven: A Neurosurgeon's Journey into the Afterlife* (New York: Simon and Schuster, 2012), 9.

34. Ibid., 148.

35. "Akiane Kramarik | Conversations at KCTS 9," http://www.youtube.com/watch?v=cYDzUTZys8g&feature =player_embedded.

36. Burpo with Vincent, *Heaven Is for Real*, 142.

37. Ibid., 138.

38. Elizabeth L. Hillstrom, *Testing the Spirits* (Downers Grove, IL: InterVarsity Press, 1995), 104.

39. Marvin J. Besteman with Lorilee Craker, *My Journey to Heaven: What I Saw and How It Changed My Life* (Grand Rapids: Revell, 2012), 12.

40. Ibid., 185.

41. Ibid., 14.

42. Ibid., 88.

43. Ibid., 100.

44. Michael Sabom, "The Shadow of Death," part 2, *Christian Research Journal*, 26, no. 3 (2003), online at http://www.equip.org/PDF/DD282-2.pdf, accessed August 15, 2012.

45. Eadie with Taylor, *Embraced by the Light*, 42.

46. Moody, *Life after Life* and Alexander, *Proof of Heaven*.

47. Mark Hitchcock, *55 Answers to Questions about Life after Death* (Sisters, OR: Multnomah, 2005), 134–35.

48. Burpo with Vincent, *Heaven Is for Real*, 103.

49. Carl Sagan, *Cosmos* (New York: Random House, 1980), 1.

50. Alexander, *Proof of Heaven*, 9.

51. Dr. Eben Alexander, "Heaven Is Real: A Doctor's Experience with the Afterlife," October 8, 2012, online at The Daily Beast website, http://www.thedailybeast.com/newsweek/2012/10/07/proof-of-heaven-a-doctor-s-experience-with-the-afterlife.html (accessed December 6, 2012).

52. Alexander, *Proof of Heaven*, 9.

53. "Are NDEs Hallucinations?" http://www.near-death.com/
    experiences/lsd04.html, accessed August 12, 2012; and Ronald
    K. Siegel, *Fire in the Brain: Clinical Tales of Hallucination* (New
    York, Dutton, 1992).

54. Susan Blackmore, *Dying to Live: Near-Death Experiences*
    (Buffalo, NY: Prometheus Books, 1993); see the excellent
    summary analysis of Blackmore's arguments in Doug Groothuis,
    Deceived by the Light (Eugene, OR: Harvest House, 1995),
    173–79.

55. Jon Trott, "The Grade Five Syndrome," *Cornerstone* 20 no. 96
    (1991): 16.

56. George Ganaway, "Historical versus Narrative Truth," *Journal of
    Dissociation* 2, no. 4 (December 1989): 205–20; Steven Jay Lynn
    and Judith W. Rhue, "Fantasy Proneness," *American Psychologist*,
    (January 1988): 35–44; and Judith W. Rhue and Steven Jay Lynn,
    "Fantasy Proneness, Hypnotizability, and Multiple Personality,"
    Human Suggestibility, ed. John F. Schumaker (New York:
    Routledge, 1991), 201.

57. Gary R. Habermas and J. P. Moreland, *Beyond Death: Exploring
    the Evidence for Immortality* (Wheaton, IL: Crossway, 1998), 52.

58. The lines of reasoning in this paragraph are clearly and cogently
    fleshed out in Habermas and Moreland, *Beyond Death*, chapter 2.

CHAPTER 8. IS THERE A TRANSITIONAL HELL?

1. Timothy R. Phillips, "Hades," in *Evangelical Dictionary of
   Biblical Theology*, ed. Walter A. Elwell (Grand Rapids: Baker,
   1996), 322.

2. *Documents of the Council of Trent*, Session VI (January 13,
   1547), "Canons Concerning Justification," Canon 30, http://
   www.catholic-forum.com/saints/trent06.htm#2.

3. *New Catholic Encyclopedia* 1979, 11:1034; see also J. F. X. Cevetello, R. J. Bastian, *New Catholic Encyclopedia* (The Gale Group, 2003), http://www.encyclopedia.com/article-1G2-3407709208/purgatory.html.

4. "Harrowing of Hell," according to *The Catholic Encyclopedia*, "is the Old English and Middle English term for the triumphant descent of Christ into hell (or Hades) between the time of his crucifixion and his resurrection, when, according to Christian belief, he brought salvation to the souls held captive there since the beginning of the world" (http://www.newadvent.org/cathen/07143d.htm). For a biblical perspective, however, see "Did Jesus go to hell?" and "Why does the Apostles' Creed say that Jesus 'descended into hell'?" in this book.

5. Richard P. McBrien, gen. ed., *The HarperCollins Encyclopedia of Catholicism* (New York: HarperSanFrancisco, 1995), 771.

6. Ibid.

7. The Barna Group, "Americans Describe Their Views about Life After Death," October 21, 2003; http://www.barna.org/barna-update/article/5-barna-update/128-americans-describe-their-views-about-life-after-death. The Barna Group also reports that one in five Americans in general believes in reincarnation.

8. John Leo, "I Was Beheaded in the 1700s," *Time* (10 September 1984): 68.

9. Frederick K. C. Price, *Ever Increasing Faith Messenger* 7 (June 1980), quoted in D. R. McConnell, *A Different Gospel*, updated edition (Peabody, MA: Hendrickson, 1995), 117.

10. Kenneth Copeland, "Jesus—Our Lord of Glory," *Believer's Voice of Victory* 10, no. 4 (April 1982): 3.

11. For a full exposition, see part 4 of my book, *Christianity in Crisis: 21st Century* (Nashville: Thomas Nelson, 2009).

12. Philip Schaff, ed., *The Creeds of Christendom with a History and Critical Notes*, vol. 1 (Grand Rapids: Baker, 1985), 16.

13. Ibid., 19.
14. Augustine, *Letter 164*, chapter 1.
15. Thomas Aquinas, *Summa Theologica*, 3.52.2.
16. John Calvin, *Institutes of the Christian Religion*, 2.16.8.
17. Schaff, *The Creeds of Christendom*, 45–46, 69.

PART 3—LIFE: WHAT YOU DO NOW COUNTS FOR ALL ETERNITY

1. For in-depth analysis concerning Daniel's prophecies of the succession of nations and the abomination that causes desolation, see Hank Hanegraaff, *Has God Spoken? Memorable Proofs of the Bible's Divine Inspiration* (Nashville: Thomas Nelson, 2011), part 3.
2. C. S. Lewis, *Mere Christianity* (New York: HarperCollins, 1952), 46.
3. N. T. Wright, *Surprised by Hope: Rethinking Heaven, the Resurrection, and the Mission of the Church* (New York: HarperOne, 2008), 202, emphasis in original.
4. Nancy R. Pearcey, *Total Truth: Liberating Christianity from Its Cultural Captivity* (Wheaton, IL: Crossway, 2004), 47.
5. Michael Weiskopf, "Energized by Pulpit or Passion, the Public Is Calling: 'Gospel Grapevine' Displays Strength in Controversy over Military Gay Ban," *The Washington Post*, February 1, 1993, A1; as quoted in Pearcey, *Total Truth*, 33.

CHAPTER 9. DOESN'T A LOVING GOD WANT EVERYONE IN HEAVEN?

1. Rob Bell, *Love Wins: A Book about Heaven, Hell, and the Fate of Every Person Who Ever Lived* (New York: HarperOne, 2011), 173, emphasis added.

2. Ibid., 174.

3. Ibid., 175.

4. J. I. Packer in Ajith Fernando, *Crucial Questions about Hell* (Wheaton, IL: Crossway Books, 1991) x–xi.

5. Bell, *Love Wins*, 1–2.

6. Ibid., 2.

7. Ibid., emphasis in original.

8. Mahatma Gandhi and Robert Elsberg, *Gandhi on Christianity* (Maryknoll, NY: Orbis Books, 1991), 66.

9. Ibid.

10. Ibid., 94. Moreover, Gandhi was not shy in setting his own subjective standard of morality: "My meaning of brahmacharya is this . . . One who has never lustful intention, who by constant attendance upon God, has become capable of lying naked with naked women, however beautiful they may be, without being in any manner whatsoever sexually excited. Such a person should be incapable of lying, incapable of intending doing harm to a single man or woman, free from anger and malice and detached" (as quoted in Stanley Wolpert, *Gandhi's Passion: The Life and Legacy of Mahatma Gandhi* [New York: Oxford University Press, 2002], 17).

11. Bell, *Love Wins*, 92.

12. Ibid., 91.

13. Ibid., 96.

14. Ibid., 106.

15. Elesha Coffman, "What Luther Said," http://www.christianitytoday.com/ch/news/2002/apr12.html.

16. Andy Crouch, quoted on back cover of Bell, *Love Wins*.

17. Greg Boyd, quoted on inside back flap, Bell, *Love Wins*.

18. Martin Luther, "A Letter to Hans von Rechenberg, 1522," in *Luther's Works, Volume 43: Devotional Writings II* (Minneapolis, MN: Augsburg Fortress Press, 1968), 54, emphasis added.

19. C. S. Lewis, *The Problem of Pain* (New York: Collier Books, 1962), 118–19.

20. C. S. Lewis, *The Great Divorce* (New York: HarperCollins, 1946, 1973), 75.

21. Phillip Yancey, *Where Is God When It Hurts?* (Grand Rapids: Zondervan, 1977), 247.

22. Centers for Disease Control and Prevention, "Suicide: Facts at a Glance" (Summer 2009), http://www.cdc.gov/violenceprevention/pdf/Suicide-DataSheet-a.pdf.

CHAPTER 10. IS THERE REALLY A RESURRECTION?

1. Facts in this paragraph are drawn from William Lane Craig's opening speech in Paul Copan, ed., *Will the Real Jesus Please Stand Up? A Debate between William Lane Craig and John Dominic Crossan* (Grand Rapids: Baker, 1998), 26–27; and from William Lane Craig, "Did Jesus Rise from the Dead?" in Michael J. Wilkins and J. P. Moreland, eds., *Jesus Under Fire* (Grand Rapids: Zondervan, 1995), 146–52.

2. William Lane Craig quoted in Lee Strobel, *The Case for Christ: A Journalist's Personal Investigation of the Evidence for Jesus* (Grand Rapids: Zondervan, 1998), 217–18, emphasis in original.

3. C. H. Dodd, "The Appearances of the Risen Christ: A study in the form criticism of the Gospels," in *More New Testament Studies* (Manchester: University of Manchester, 1968), 128, quoted in William Lane Craig, *Reasonable Faith: Christian Truth and Apologetics*, 3rd ed. (Wheaton, IL: Crossway, 2008), 379.

4. Simon Greenleaf, *The Testimony of the Evangelists: The Gospels Examined by the Rules of Evidence* (Grand Rapids: Kregel Classics, 1995; originally published 1874), 31–32.

5. "International Cremation Statistics 2009," The Cremation Society of Great Britain, http://www.srgw.demon.co.uk/

CremSoc5/Stats/Interntl/2009/StatsIF.html; and "Cremation Statistics," Cremation Association of America, http://www. cremationassociation.org/?page=IndustryStatistics (both sites accessed November 8, 2012).

6. Augustine, *City of God*, 11.21.

CHAPTER 11. WHAT ABOUT THE END TIMES?

1. Tim LaHaye and Jerry B. Jenkins, *The Indwelling: The Beast Takes Possession* (Wheaton, IL: Tyndale, 2000), 367.
2. Tim LaHaye and Thomas Ice, *Charting the End Times* (Eugene, OR: Harvest House, 2001), 56, 63.
3. Ibid., 58.
4. Tim LaHaye and Jerry B. Jenkins, *Are We Living in the End Times?* (Wheaton, IL: Tyndale, 1999), 146.

CHAPTER 12. HOW DOES THE AFTERLIFE AFFECT MY LIFE NOW?

1. Watchman Nee, *The Normal Christian Life* (Peabody, MA: Hendrickson, 2010; originally published 1961).

GLOSSARY

Abraham's bosom (or Abraham's side): an expression used in the Bible only by Jesus in the parable of Lazarus and the rich man, in which a lowly righteous man (Lazarus) dies and is taken to a place of blessedness called "Abraham's bosom," and an unrighteous rich man dies and is taken to a place of torment called "hades," and an untraversable gulf separates them (Luke 16:19–31; cf. 4 Maccabees 13:17). The background is found in the Old Testament. Upon death a Jewish person went to "be with his fathers" (Genesis 15:15; 47:30; Deuteronomy 31:16). In particular, they were gathered to "father Abraham" (Luke 16:24, 27, 30), who is the father of the Jews (Luke 3:8; John 8:37–40; cf. Genesis 12).

ad hoc: (Latin, "for this") an unwarranted explanation; the addition of unjustified premises to an argument in order to preserve the argument.

annihilationism: a view of the afterlife according to which those persons who persist in refusing God's gracious gift of salvation do not spend eternity in torment in hell, but rather are annihilated or destroyed (i.e., they cease to exist entirely) at or shortly after the last judgment; annihilationism is closely associated with the notion of conditional immortality and sometimes goes by that name.

apocalyptic/apocalypse: (Greek *apocálypsis*, an unveiling) a literary genre used to describe prophetic literature composed in the highly metaphorical and symbolic language system used within postexilic Judaism and early Christianity. The book of Revelation is an apocalypse—not just in the sense of an unveiling but in the sense of what might best be described as a language system or matrix that is deeply embedded in the Old Testament canon. To comprehend Revelation, one must first understand well the rest of the Bible. (See apocalyptic prophecy.)

apocalyptic prophecy: A category of prophetic pronouncement concerned with the eschatological hope in God's blessing and vindication of the redeemed, and His righteous judgment of the wicked. It often employs hyperbolic cosmic imagery (e.g., darkening sun, blood-red moon, stars falling from the sky, foreboding clouds) and fantasy imagery (e.g., red dragons with seven heads, locusts with human faces, leopards with bear's feet and lion's teeth) to invest earthly, historical, sociopolitical events with their full theological and eternal significance.

Beatific Vision: seeing God in Christ "face to face" after death (1 Corinthians 13:12)—the direct, unmediated knowing and loving of God in life after life, and life *after* life-after-life.

canon: the thirty-nine received books of the Old Testament and the twenty-seven of the New Testament officially recognized as inspired Holy Scripture by the early Christian church (from the Greek word *kanon*, meaning "measuring rod" or "rule").

cremation: the incineration or complete burning of a corpse to ashes; an increasingly common means of disposing of a corpse despite the Bible's preference for burial and the preservation of bones.

desolation: state of complete ruin; devastation; emptiness.

dispensationalism: an eschatological viewpoint according to which God has two distinct peoples (the church and national, ethnic Israel) with two distinct plans and two distinct destinies. Dispensationalism (or dispensational theology) is distinctive for its teaching that the Church will be "raptured" from the earth in the first phase of Christ's second coming so that God can return to his work with national Israel, which was put on hold after Israel's rejection of the Messiah. God's renewed working with Israel is thought by many dispensationalists to include a seven-year period of tribulation under Antichrist in which two-thirds of the Jewish people will be killed, followed by the second phase of Christ's second coming in which Christ and the martyred "tribulation saints" will rule for a thousand years from a rebuilt temple with a reinstituted sacrificial system. Dispensationalism was first conceived by John Nelson Darby in the nineteenth century and popularized by prophecy pundits such as Hal Lindsey and Tim LaHaye in the twentieth century.

eschatology: (from the Greek word *eschatos*, meaning "last, farthest," and *logos*, "speaking, word") the study of last things or end times. Far from being a mere branch in the theological tree, eschatology is the root that provides life and luster to every fiber of its being. To study Scripture is to study eschatology, for all of God's work in redemption—past, present, and future—moves toward eternal redemption. Put another way, eschatology is the thread that weaves the tapestry of Scripture into a harmonious pattern.

eternal life: The quality and never-ending duration of knowing God in Christ, which begins at the moment of salvation (John 3:15–16, 36; 5:24; 17:3).

exegete: (noun) a person skilled in the art and science of interpreting a text, especially the Bible. As a verb it means to interpret or analyze a text thoroughly.

gehenna: (Greek) the most common word for hell in the New Testament. Synonomous with "punishment of eternal fire" (Jude 7) and "lake of fire" (Revelation 19:20 KJV; 20:14–15).

gospel of the second chance (a.k.a. postmortem evangelism): a term referring to the unbiblical view that many or all unbelievers will be granted an opportunity to receive Christ after they die and in so doing be saved.

hades: Greek word for the abode of the dead, often mistranslated as hell; the transitional hell.

heaven: the abode of God, his holy angels, and the souls of righteous people who have died; currently Christ is the only embodied being in heaven, but heaven and earth will one day become one in the resurrection and restoration of all things.

hell: the destination of eternal, conscious, and inconsolable torment that awaits Satan, rebellious angels, and unrighteous people.

heresy: a teaching that denies the essential tenets of the historic Christian faith as codified in the great, ancient ecumenical Creeds, such as the Apostles' Creed, Nicene Creed, or Creed of Athanasius.

hermeneutics: In Greek mythology, the task of the god Hermes was to interpret the will of the gods. In biblical hermeneutics, the task is to interpret the Word of God. Simply stated, hermeneutics is the art and science of biblical interpretation. It is a science in that certain rules apply. It is an art in that the more you apply these rules, the better you get at it.

imago Dei: (Latin, "image of God") that resemblance to God in which humans were originally created (Genesis 1:26–27) and which was severely impaired in the fall (Genesis 3). The image of God in humans is metaphysical, including intellect, will, and emotions; and it is ethical, including righteousness and holiness. The ethical aspects of the imago Dei were lost altogether in the first sin, while the metaphysical aspects remain in broken measure. But the imago Dei will be fully restored in Christ.

indulgences: within the complex theology of Roman Catholicism, in response to particular prayers or good works, the remission of the temporal punishment due to sin, the guilt of which has already been forgiven by God through the Church.

intermediate state: the disembodied state of existence that humans experience between the moments of physical death and resurrection.

libertarian freedom: the ability to will and to act in alternative ways, unconstrained by any external determining factors; freedom of the will.

limbo: according to a prominent and, until recently, officially endorsed Roman Catholic view, the eternal dwelling place of babies who die before being baptized. In limbo, unbaptized babies enjoy a good life but do not enjoy the most intimate knowledge of God, referred to as the Beatific Vision, which is a state of blessedness reserved for baptized Christians.

materialist: a proponent of materialism, the belief that only material entities exist such that a comprehensive physical theory within science could, in principle, explain all of reality.

millennium: a thousand-year period mentioned in chapter 20 of the book of Revelation. Though mistaken by many as a semi-golden age of Christian history—leading to much debate over whether the return of Christ will happen before (premillennialism) or after (postmillennialism) the millennium, or whether the millennium is symbolic of the period of time between Christ's first and second advents (amillennialism)—the thousand years of Revelation are symbolic of the vindication enjoyed by the martyrs who died under the first-century persecution of the Beast.

near-death experience (NDE): the subjective recollection of an experience that occurred during a state of unconsciousness precipitated by a medical crisis such as an accident, suicide attempt, or a cardiac arrest.

numerically identical: the same thing; to say that Christ's resurrected body is numerically identical to his body that died on the cross is to say that the very body that expired on the cross is the body in which he rose again from the dead, not another body.

Olivet Discourse: the prophetic and apocalyptic sermon Jesus delivered on the Mount of Olives in which he lamented Israel's rebellion against God and prophesied that he would bring judgment on Jerusalem before the generation of his contemporaries had passed away—a prophecy unambiguously fulfilled in AD 70 when the Roman army utterly destroyed the temple and the city. Parallel accounts of the Olivet Discourse are found in Matthew 24–25, Mark 13, and Luke 21.

omnipotent: literally, "all-powerful"; God, and God alone, is able to do anything that is logically possible and consistent with his nature. It is no weakness in God that he cannot, for example, cease to exist; for a necessary being (a being that cannot not exist, such as God) is greater than a contingent being (a being that could have not existed, such as you and I).

omnipresent: literally "all present"; God and God alone is able to be present everywhere at the same time, not in the sense of being physically distributed throughout the universe, according to philosophical theologian William Lane Craig, but in the sense that although God exists spacelessly he has direct knowledge of and is causally active at every point in space.

omniscient: literally, "all-knowing"; God, and God alone, knows everything there is to know—and he knows everything directly, not by observation or inference. No creature will ever attain omniscience.

Paradise: when capitalized, this term refers to the garden of Eden, before the fall of Adam and Eve. Not to be confused with **paradise** (Abraham's bosom) or **paradise restored** (the eternal heavens and earth).

paradise (a.k.a. Abraham's bosom or Abraham's side): the domain of God's loving presence into which believers enter at death—the spiritual realm of life after life.

paradise restored: the final consummation of all things—the resurrection and restoration of all of creation in life *after* life-after-life.

philosophical naturalism: the worldview that nothing exists except the natural world, and all of nature is in principle entirely explainable in terms of science (physics and chemistry). This worldview is well codified in the famous aphorism of the late atheist astronomer Carl Sagan: "The Cosmos is all that is or ever was or ever will be."

pretext: a false premise or assumption that takes the place of the true meaning or intention. To say that "a text without a context is a pretext" is to say that the real meaning of the passage in question has been supplanted by a notion that the author never intended to communicate because contextual information essential to discerning the real meaning has been excluded.

purgatory: in Roman Catholicism, the intermediate state after death in which persons who were justified and reconciled in Christ prior to death but have not received temporal punishment for their sins in the process of sanctification are fully purified and made fit to see God in heaven.

quarantine: deliberate separation from others.

reincarnation: the dogma of many non-Christian Eastern religions that at physical death the soul reenters the cycle of rebirth rather than, as in Christianity, entering into the transitional disembodied state (bliss or torment) followed by the final resurrection state (heaven or hell).

replacement theologian: 1. "the pejorative label given by dispensational writers to those who hold the view that the promises made by God to Abraham and his 'seed' are now fulfilled in Christ to the church, which is the new Israel. In other words, the church 'replaces' Israel in God's covenant plan. On this view, ethnic Israel has no special covenantal claims apart from Christ. The Jew as well as the Gentile must become a part of the body of Christ through conversion in order to enjoy any covenantal standing with God. It seems to me that the New Testament declares these things in unmistakable terms (e.g., Romans 2:28–29; Galatians 3:16, 29; 4:22–31; Philippians 3:3), and never mentions any future blessings that are to accrue to ethnic Israel outside of the church. . . . ([This was] the view of the church fathers, of the Medieval Church, of the Reformers, of most modern Reformed Christians and many other evangelicals)" (Steve Gregg, "Looking for America in All the Wrong Places," *Christian Research Journal*, 28, no. 1 [2005]), accessible online at http://www.equip.org/PDF/JAE151.pdf). 2. denotatively, replacement theology is the dispensational belief that national Israel will replace the church as the focus of God's plan during a seven-year period of tribulation.

resurrection: the raising of a body from death to eternal life; used to refer to the general resurrection of the dead—the just to eternal life and the wicked to eternal separation from God—that will occur at the time of Christ's future bodily return to earth (John 5:28–29, 1 Corinthians 15, 1 Thessalonians 4); also used to refer to Jesus' resurrection from the dead as "the firstfruits of those who have fallen asleep" (1 Corinthians 15:20).

salvation: the rescue of sinners from the wrath of the living and holy God by grace alone, through faith alone, on account of Christ alone (Ephesians 2).

sanctification: in theology, the process whereby, through cooperation with God in Christ, the justified and saved individual is transformed by the Holy Spirit into the image of Christ, becoming intrinsically righteous; in contrast to the doctrine of sanctification, the doctrine of forensic justification is that by grace alone, through faith alone, on account of Christ alone, God imputes or accredits to the believer the righteousness of Christ, independently of any change that takes place within the individual. In justification, God forgives and reconciles the sinner to himself and grants the sinner eternal life solely in virtue of Christ's imputed righteousness, on account of Christ's perfect fulfillment of God's law (active obedience) and his death on the cross (passive obedience) on the sinner's behalf. Sinners are justified before God and saved from His coming wrath through no work of their own, but solely by grace alone, through faith alone, on account of Christ alone. Justification is immediate at the point of conversion to faith in Christ; but sanctification is a life-long process not completed until the consummation of all things on the last day in resurrection and glorification. The doctrine of justification is aptly captured in Martin Luther's coarse analogy that the believer in Christ is like snow-covered dung. But it is through sanctification that the believer becomes intrinsically righteous and Christlike.

scriptorture: When we trip over another bit of Scripture that should modify our thinking. Instead of conforming our opinion to Scripture, we beat the opposing Scripture passage into submission so that it fits our previous conception because we've grown comfortable with our old position and don't want to change.

secular humanist: a person whose worldview is characterized by atheism (denial of the existence of any supernatural deity), naturalism (the natural world exhausts reality), usually ethical relativism (denial of the existence of objective morals and values), and the abject rejection of any form of religious faith and practice (except the religion of secular humanism).

sensationalism: exploitation of stirring or shocking stories or ideas, regardless of accuracy, in order to arouse interest.

Shekinah: the radiant presence or glory of God—the external manifestation of God's being—dwelling with his people (Exodus 16:10; Numbers 14:22; Isaiah 40:5; cf. Exodus 25:8; 29:45–46).

sin: that which causes a break in relationship with God or fails to meet God's standard of perfection. Sin is not just murder, rape, or robbery, but it is failing to do the things we should and doing those things that we should not. In short, sin is the barrier between you and a satisfying relationship with God. Just as light and dark cannot exist together, neither can God and sin.

somatic: of, or having to do with a physical body (from the Greek word *soma*, meaning "body").

soul sleep: the view that between death and the general resurrection, the soul continues to exist but in a state of unconsciousness; this view is held by a small minority of Christians, including Seventh-day Adventists. Relatedly, a growing minority of Christians influenced by the scientism of our day embrace what is called Christian or non-reductive physicalism, which denies the existence of a substantive immaterial soul altogether, such that upon death the individual simply ceases to exist but will be "resurrected" (i.e., re-created) by God on the last day.

transitional heaven: the intermediate state as experienced by those who are dead in Christ; a disembodied state of great joy in the presence of God awaiting the resurrection; paradise.

typology (type, antitype): A type (from the Greek word *typos*, meaning "impression, model, or image") is a person, event, or institution in the redemptive history of the Old Testament that prefigures a corresponding but greater reality in the New Testament. A type is thus a copy, pattern, or model that signifies a greater reality. The greater reality to which a type points, and in which it finds its fulfillment, is referred to as an *antitype* (from the Greek word *antitypos*, meaning "corresponding to something that has gone before").

universalism: a view of the afterlife according to which all people end up in heaven for eternity, though some may have to endure a brief period of punishment or painful purification.

wax nose: someone or something malleable and readily influenced; thus, to turn the Scriptures into a wax nose is to read into them what is not there (eisegesis), rather than drawing out from them the meaning the author intended (exegesis).

worldview: the collection of a person's most fundamental beliefs about the world, together with one's dispositions that guide her or his perception and understanding of the world.

Word of Faith: Some of America's best-known televangelists subscribe either partly or wholly to what's commonly referred to as "positive confession," the "Word-Faith" teaching, or the "prosperity" doctrine. The basic teaching may be summarized as follows: God created man in "God's class," as "little gods," with the potential to exercise what they refer to as the "God-kind of faith" in calling things into existence and living in prosperity and success as sovereign beings. Of course, we forfeited this opportunity by rebelling against God in the Garden and taking upon ourselves Satan's nature. To correct this situation, Jesus Christ became a man, died spiritually (thus taking upon himself Satan's nature), went to hell, was "born again," rose from the dead with God's nature again, and then sent the Holy Spirit so that the incarnation could be duplicated in believers, thus fulfilling their calling to be what they call "little gods." Since we are all called to experience this kind of life now, we should be successful in virtually every area of our lives. To be in debt, then, or be sick, or (as is even taught by the faith teachers) to be left by one's spouse, simply means that you don't have enough faith—or you have some secret sin in your life, because if you didn't, you would be able to handle all of these problems.

FOR FURTHER STUDY

SOMEDAY YOU WILL DIE—THEN WHAT?

Wright, N. T. *Surprised by Hope: Rethinking Heaven, the Resurrection, and the Mission of the Church*. New York: HarperOne, 2008.

PART ONE

Life *after* Life-after-Life: The Eternal Heaven and Earth

CHAPTER 1. WHAT IS HEAVEN ABOUT?

Eareckson Tada, Joni. *Heaven: Your Real Home*. Grand Rapids: Zondervan, 1995.

Wright, N. T. *Surprised by Hope: Rethinking Heaven, the Resurrection, and the Mission of the Church*. New York: HarperOne, 2008.

CHAPTER 2. WHAT HAPPENS TO US IN HEAVEN?

Habermas, Gary R., and J. P. Moreland. *Beyond Death: Exploring the Evidence for Immortality*. Wheaton, IL: Crossway Books, 1998.

Kreeft, Peter J. *Everything You Ever Wanted to Know about Heaven, but Never Dreamed of Asking*. San Francisco: Ignatius Press, 1990.

CHAPTER 3. WHAT IS HEAVEN LIKE?

Hanegraaff, Hank. *Resurrection*. Nashville: W Publishing Group, a division of Thomas Nelson, 2000.

Lewis, C. S. *Miracles*. New York: Harper Collins, 1974.

For advanced study see:

Craig, William Lane. *Time and Eternity: Exploring God's Relationship to Time*. Wheaton, IL: Crossway, 2001.

CHAPTER 4. WHAT'S UP WITH HELL?

Blanchard, John. *Whatever Happened to Hell?* Wheaton, IL: Crossway Books, 1995.

Habermas, Gary R., and J. P. Moreland. *Beyond Death: Exploring the Evidence for Immortality*. Wheaton, IL.: Crossway Books, 1998.

Morgan, Christopher W., and Robert A. Peterson, ed. *Hell Under Fire: Modern Scholarship Reinvents Eternal Punishment*. Grand Rapids: Zondervan, 2001.

Peterson, Robert A. *Hell on Trial: The Case for Eternal Punishment*. Phillipsburg, NJ: P&R Publishing, 1995.

PART TWO

Life after Life: The Transitional Heaven

CHAPTER 5. WHAT HAPPENS TO US BETWEEN DEATH AND HEAVEN?

Cooper, John W. *Body, Soul, & Life Everlasting: Biblical Anthropology and the Monism-Dualism Debate*. Grand Rapids: Eerdmans, 1989.

Habermas, Gary R., and J. P. Moreland. *Beyond Death: Exploring the Evidence for Immortality*. Wheaton, IL: Crossway, 1998.

CHAPTER 6. WHAT IS THE TRANSITIONAL HEAVEN LIKE?

Beckwith, Francis. "Philosophical Problems with the Mormon Concept of God." *Christian Research Journal* 14, no. 4 (Spring 1992): 24–29. Available at http://www.equip.org/articles/philosophical-problems-with-the-mormon-concept-of-god/

Onken, Brian. "The Atonement of Christ and the Faith Message," *Forward* 7, no. 1 (1984): 1, 10–15. Available at http://www.equip.org/articles/the-atonement-of-christ-and-the-faith-message/

Farrow, Douglas. *Ascension and Ecclesia: On the Significance of the Doctrine of the Ascension for Ecclesiology and Christian Cosmology.* Grand Rapids: Eerdmans, 1999.

Moreland, J. P. and William Lane Craig. *Philosophical Foundations for a Christian Worldview.* Downers Grove, IL: IVP Academic, 2003.

CHAPTER 7. ARE NEAR-DEATH EXPERIENCES THE REAL THING?

Abanes, Richard. *Journey into the Light: Exploring Near-Death Experiences.* Grand Rapids: Baker, 1996.

Groothuis, Douglas. "Deceived by the Light: A Christian Response to *Embraced by the Light.*" *Christian Research Journal* 18, no. 2 (Fall 1995): 24ff. Available at http://www.equip.org/PDF/DE305.pdf

Hillstrom, Elizabeth L. *Testing the Spirits.* Downers Grove, IL: InterVarsity Press, 1995.

Yamamoto, J. Isamu. "The Near Death Experience: The New Age Connection (Part 1)" *Christian Research Journal* (Spring 1992): 20–23. Available at http://www.equip.org/PDF/DT082-1.pdf
_____. "The Near-Death Experience: Alternative Explanations (Part 2)." *Christian Research Journal* (Summer 1992): 14–24. Available at http://www.equip.org/articles/the-near-death-experience-part-two/

CHAPTER 8. IS THERE A TRANSITIONAL HELL?

Blanchard, John. *Whatever Happened to Hell?* Wheaton, IL: Crossway, 1995.

Cooper, John W. *Body, Soul, & Life Everlasting: Biblical Anthropology and the Monism-Dualism Debate*. Grand Rapids: Eerdmans, 1989.

Hanegraaff, Hank. *Christianity in Crisis: 21st Century*. Nashville: Thomas Nelson, 2009.

Mayhall, C. Wayne. "Worse than a 'Vale of Tears': Karma in the Shadow of the Cross." *Christian Research Institute* 30, no. 3 (2007): 34–43. Available at http://www.equip.org/PDF/JAK060.pdf

Montenegro, Marcia. "I See Dead People." *Christian Research Journal* 25, no. 1 (2002): 10–19. Available at http://www.equip.org/articles/i-see-dead-people/

Rogers, Gregory. "Does John 3:3 Support Reincarnation?" *Christian Research Journal* 30, no. 4 (2007):50–51. Available at http://www.equipresources.org/atf/cf/%7B9C4EE03A-F988-4091-84BD-F8E70A3B0215%7D/JAR133.pdf

PART THREE

Life: What You Do Now Counts for All Eternity

CHAPTER 9. DOESN'T A LOVING GOD WANT EVERYONE IN HEAVEN?

Cable, Matthew. "Funeral Faux Pas." *Christian Research Journal* 29, no. 2 (2006): 10–11. Available at http://www.equip.org/articles/funeral-faux-pas/

Groothuis, Douglas. *"Love Wins*: Making a Contradictory Case for Universalism." *Christian Research Journal* 34, no. 4 (2011): 44–51. Available at http://www.equip.org/articles/love-wins-making-a-contradictory-case-for-universalism/

Habermas, Gary R., and J. P. Moreland. *Beyond Death: Exploring the Evidence for Immortality*. Wheaton, IL: Crossway, 1998.

Hunter, Bob. "Carlton Pearson's Gospel of Inclusion." *Christian Research Journal* 30, no. 4 (2007): 17. Available at http://www.equipresources.org/atf/cf/%7B9C4EE03A-F988-4091-84BD-F8E70A3B0215%7D/JAH192.pdf

Mayhall, C. Wayne. "Suicide: Answering Against Eternity." *Christian Research Journal* 31, no. 3 (2008): 10–19. Available at http://www.equip.org/articles/suicide-answering-against-eternity/

Miller, Elliot. "Thinking about the Unthinkable." *Christian Research Journal* 31, no. 3 (2008): 3. Available at http://www.equip.org/articles/thinking-about-the-unthinkable/

Nash, Ronald. "Is Belief in Jesus Necessary? The Answer to Religious Inclusivism." *Christian Research Journal* 27, no. 3 (2004): 22–30. Available at http://www.equip.org/articles/is-belief-in-jesus-necessary/

———. "Is Jesus the Only Savior? The Answer to Religious Pluralism." *Christian Research Journal* 27, no. 2 (2004): 22–31. Available at http://www.equip.org/PDF/JAJ771.pdf

———. *Is Jesus the Only Savior?* Grand Rapids: Zondervan, 1994.

———. "Is There Salvation after Death? The Answer to Postmortem Evangelism." *Christian Research Journal* 27, no. 4 (2004): 32–40. Available at http://www.equip.org/PDF/JAJ773.pdf

CHAPTER 10. IS THERE REALLY A RESURRECTION?

Aquinas, Thomas. *Summa Theologica*. QQ 50–64.

Beckwith, Francis J. "God Knows?" *Christian Research Journal* 22, no. 4 (2000): 54–56. Available at http://www.equip.org/PDF/DG237.pdf

Beilby, James K., and Paul R. Eddy, eds. *Divine Foreknowledge: Four Views*. Downers Grove, IL: InterVarsity Press, 2001. The views defended by David Hunt, William Lane Craig, and Paul Helm are within the pale of historic Christian orthodoxy.

Craig, William Lane. *Reasonable Faith: Christian Truth and Apologetics*, 3rd ed. Wheaton, IL: Crossway, 2008.

Habermas, Gary R., and Michael R. Licona. *The Case for the Resurrection of Jesus*. Grand Rapids: Kregel, 2004.

Hanegraaff, Hank. *Has God Spoken? Memorable Proofs of the Bible's Divine Inspiration*. Nashville: Thomas Nelson, 2011.

_____. *Resurrection*. Nashville: W Publishing, 2000.

Huffman, Douglas S., and Eric L. Johnson, eds. *God Under Fire: Modern Scholarship Reinvents God*. Grand Rapids: Zondervan, 2002.

For advanced study see:

Licona, Michael R. *The Resurrection of Jesus: A New Historiographical Approach*. Downers Grove, IL: IVP Academic, 2010.

Wright, N. T. *The Resurrection of the Son of God*. Minneapolis: Fortress, 2003.

CHAPTER 11. WHAT ABOUT THE END TIMES?

Bauckham, Richard. *The Theology of the Book of Revelation*. Cambridge, UK: University of Cambridge, 1993.

Clouse, Robert G., ed. *The Meaning of the Millennium: Four Views*. Downers Grove, IL: InterVarsity Press, 1977.

DeMar, Gary. *Is Jesus Coming Soon?* Powder Springs, GA: American Vision, 2006.

Gregg, Steve. *Revelation: Four Views—A Parallel Commentary*. Nashville: Thomas Nelson, 1997.

Hanegraaff, Hank. *Has God Spoken? Memorable Proofs of the Bible's Divine Inspiration*. Nashville: Thomas Nelson, 2011.

———. *The Apocalypse Code: Find Out What the Bible Really Says about the End Times and Why It Matters Today.* Nashville: Thomas Nelson, 2007.

Sproul, R. C. *The Last Days According to Jesus: When Did Jesus Say He Would Return?* Grand Rapids: Baker, 1998.

CHAPTER 12. HOW DOES THE AFTERLIFE AFFECT MY LIFE NOW?

MacArthur, John. *Hard to Believe: The High Cost and Infinite Value of Following Jesus.* Nashville: Thomas Nelson, 2003.

Nee, Watchman. *The Normal Christian Life.* Peabody, MA: Hendrickson, 1961.

Strobel, Lee. "The Circumstantial Evidence: Are There Any Supporting Facts that Point to the Resurrection? with Dr. J. P. Moreland," in *The Case for Christ: A Journalist's Personal Investigation of the Evidence for Jesus.* Grand Rapids: Zondervan, 1998.

Whitney, Donald. *Spiritual Disciples for the Christian Life.* Colorado Springs: NavPress, 1991.

Willard, Dallas. *The Spirit of the Disciplines: Understanding How God Changes Lives.* New York: HarperCollins, 1991.

ABOUT THE AUTHOR

Hendrik (Hank) Hanegraaff serves as president and chairman of the board of the North Carolina–based Christian Research Institute. He is also host of the nationally syndicated *Bible Answer Man* radio broadcast, which is heard daily across the United States and Canada—and around the world via the Internet at www.equip.org.

Widely regarded as one of the world's leading Christian authors and apologists, Hank is deeply committed to equipping Christians to be so familiar with truth that when counterfeits loom on the horizon, they recognize them instantaneously. Through his live call-in radio broadcast, Hank equips Christians to read the Bible for all its worth, answers questions on the basis of careful research and sound reasoning, and interviews today's most significant leaders, apologists, and thinkers.

Hank is the author of more than twenty books, which have cumulatively sold millions of copies. *Christianity in Crisis* and *Resurrection* each won the Gold Medallion for Excellence in Christian Literature awarded by the Evangelical Christian Publisher's Association (ECPA); and *Counterfeit Revival* and *The FACE that Demonstrates the Farce of Evolution* each won ECPA's Silver Medallion—the latter published in the condensed *Fatal Flaws: What Evolutionists Don't Want You to Know*.

Other noteworthy volumes include *The Prayer of Jesus*, which rose to number one on the Christian Marketplace Bestseller list October 2002, and the popular *Complete Bible Answer Book—Collector's Edition*, which clearly and concisely answers common questions regarding Christianity, culture, and cults, while tackling complex questions

including, "How can Christians legitimize a God who orders the geno-
cide of entire nations?" and "Does the Bible promote slavery?"

Hank exposes the dangers of both Christian and secular Zionism
through his groundbreaking *The Apocalypse Code: What the Bible
Really Teaches about the End Times and Why It Matters Today*, and
his historical fiction series The Last Disciple Trilogy, including the
recently released third volume *The Last Temple*, as well as *Fuse of
Armageddon*.

In *Has God Spoken?* Hank provides memorable proofs for the Bible's
divine inspiration. Additional works include *The Legacy Study Bible*,
The Covering: God's Plan to Protect You from Evil, and *The Creation
Answer Book*.

He is a regular contributor to the award-winning *Christian Research
Journal* and an articulate communicator on the pressing issues of our
day, having spoken in leading churches, conferences, and on college
campuses throughout the world (most recently, the University of
Tehran, Iran).

Hank and his wife, Kathy, live in Charlotte, North Carolina, and are
parents to twelve children.

WORTHY

PUBLISHING

IF YOU ENJOYED THIS BOOK, WILL YOU CONSIDER SHARING THE MESSAGE WITH OTHERS?

- Mention the book in a Facebook post, Twitter update, Pinterest pin, or blog post.

- Recommend this book to those in your small group, book club, workplace, and classes.

- Head over to facebook.com/worthypublishing, "LIKE" the page, and post a comment as to what you enjoyed the most.

- Tweet "I recommend reading #AfterLife"

- Pick up a copy for someone you know who would be challenged and encouraged by this message.

- Write a review on amazon.com or bn.com.

You can subscribe to Worthy Publishing's newsletter at **www.worthypublishing.com.**

WORTHY PUBLISHING
FACEBOOK PAGE

WORTHY PUBLISHING
WEBSITE